COPING WITH PARENTS

by
JEROME HELLMUTH

THE ROSEN PUBLISHING GROUP
New York

Published in 1985 by The Rosen Publishing Group, Inc.
29 East 21st Street, New York City, New York 10010

First Edition

Library of Congress Cataloging in Publication Data

Hellmuth, Jerome.
   Coping with parents.

   1. Parents. I. Title.
HQ755.8.H45 1985   646.7′8   84–24873
ISBN 0–8239–0640–X

Manufactured in the United States of America

Dedicated
to the new generation of parents, who,
I hope, will find this book useful

About the Author

Jerome Hellmuth is the director of the Bucklin Hill School, a residential farm school for mentally handicapped adolescents in Bainbridge Island, Washington.

He has been a teacher in junior and senior high schools in Winnetka, Illinois, and Lake Placid, New York. At the Elisabeth Irwin High School in New York, he taught and served successively as Assistant Director and Director of Guidance. As a psychotherapist, he maintained a private practice and served as counselor at the Madison House and Hudson Guild settlement houses.

Moving to Washington State, Hellmuth taught in the Seattle Public Schools and was teacher and art therapist at the King County Juvenile Court Detention Center. Subsequently he was Director of the School for the Special Child and the Seattle Seguin School for brain-damaged and mentally handicapped children, both in Seattle. He is the author of *A Wolf in the Family* and is Editor and Co-Publisher of Special Child Publications, Seattle.

Contents

	Introduction	vii
I.	*Parents Begin with a Love Story*	1
II.	*To Love Is to Live Together*	4
III.	*Learning to Love and Live Together*	8
IV.	*Why Have a Baby?*	11
V.	*How Does a Parent Learn to Be a Parent?*	16
VI.	*Raising Kids*	20
VII.	*Parents of the Handicapped*	23
VIII.	*Schooling*	28
IX.	*Playing Favorites*	32
X.	*The Communication Gap*	36
XI.	*Parent Panic Over Adolescents*	40
XII.	*Are Mothers and Fathers Different?*	43
XIII.	*Parent Personalities*	47
XIV.	*Can Parents Be Bad for You?*	51
XV.	*Do Parents Make Good Friends?*	55
XVI.	*Working Mothers*	58
XVII.	*Who Holds the Purse Strings?*	62
XVIII.	*Parents as Citizens*	66
XIX.	*Parents Don't Stay the Same*	69
XX.	*When Tragedy Strikes*	73
XXI.	*When Parents Stop Loving Each Other*	76
XXII.	*Infidelity*	80
XXIII.	*Divorce*	83
XXIV.	*New Moms and Dads*	87
XXV.	*The Single Parent*	89
XXVI.	*Kids Grow Up, Parents Grow Old*	92
XXVII.	*What Happens to Old Parents?*	96
XXVIII.	*The Death of Parents*	100
XXIX.	*The Legacy of Parents*	104
XXX.	*Is the Influence of Parents Slipping?*	108
XXXI.	*How Do Your Parents Stand?*	111
	Appendix: Where and How To Get Help	113

Introduction

Everyone has parents. Parents make up the most important part of the population, for if it weren't for parents the human race would soon come to an end.

But parents do more than just keep the human race alive by populating the world with future generations. They also mold the mind of the human race by their great influence on the child from the moment it is born until it is old enough to leave home and take care of itself. That means that for a good part of our life we are totally dependent on our parents for what we eat, think, and do. What happens to us is mostly up to them. We are in their hands for better or worse.

Because of the great importance of parents in our lives, they deserve more study and attention than they receive from you, the kids who are living with them.

It is surprising how little kids know about parents, but that is not through any fault of theirs. Parents just don't tell kids what they should know about parents. The personal life of parents has always been made forbidden territory.

It is also a common belief that kids don't have the capacity to understand parents. Then, many grownups don't see any need to tell kids what kind of people parents are. They believe kids should keep their noses out of parents' business, that they should wait until they become parents to understand parents.

But what is the good of that? If kids are to get along with parents they must be given the chance to understand them while they are still living with them, not after they have grown up and left home. If they were given this understanding when they needed it, it might save many of them, as adults, from spending painful hours and a lot of money going to psychiatrists trying to straighten out what they weren't allowed to understand as kids.

Parents often say, "I just can't understand my kids." Well, kids can say the same thing about parents.

Thousands of books have been written by all kinds of

experts telling parents how they can better understand their kids. Few, if any, books have been written for kids on how to understand their parents.

At home kids are constantly scrutinized and judged by parents. In school they are graded on everything they do and given all kinds of tests to see how they shape up and what makes them tick.

It is the purpose of this book to give you, the kids, an equal chance to know about parents, especially your own parents, as they have had to learn about you. The book may not cover everything you should know or would like to know about parents. What is more important, it will enable you to participate in finding some of the answers yourself. If possible, the book should be read together with your parents. At the end of each chapter are a number of questions suggested for discussion with your parents. These, along with any you may have, should stimulate an informative dialogue to help you gain a better understanding of parents, especially your own.

You may ask, "What good is it to know about parents?" A fair question. If you want to know what kind of kid you are, or what kind of person you may become when you are an adult, you'd better start knowing more about parents, especially your own. Whether you like it or not, you become pretty much what your parents *did* or *did not* do *for* or *to* you during all those years you lived with them.

That holds true for so-called substitute or surrogate parents. You may have been adopted as a baby or have always lived with stepparents or in a foster or group home. What they did or did not do for or to you will also determine what kind of kid you are now and what kind of adult you may be in the future.

The better you know your parents, especially your own parents, whether they be real or surrogate, the better you will know yourself and help yourself to be a better person. Perhaps, too, this book will help you, if you so choose when the time comes, to be the kind of person you believe a parent should be.

CHAPTER I

Parents Begin with a Love Story

Before there is marriage or children, there is first a love story. It is the story of boy meets girl, of two young persons who fall in love with each other and want to share their lives together. It is a time when nothing in the world matters to them but their love for each other.

Most of you know very little about this early love story of your parents, since it took place before you were born and you may never have been told about it. Yet it could be the most important love story for you to know. Much of what you are today and may be for the rest of your life flows from the very special love your parents had for each other before you came into their lives.

How two persons like your parents fell in love with each other is not always easy to explain; it is such a deep personal experience that even the greatest poets find it hard to express. If you were to ask your parents, they might not be able to explain it very well either. Still, it is important that you try to find out from them something about the love they had for each other when they were young.

At your high school age today you may not be too far from the age of your parents when they first fell in love. In fact, you may now be in love yourself and experiencing some of the feelings your parents had for each other when they were first in love. This close identification with your parents as young lovers can perhaps give you a fresh perspective on them.

Why is the early love of parents so important? Because that early love, if not carefully nurtured and protected in the years that follow, will not survive to nourish them or their children. Without it the family falls apart, and what follows is sad but

1

all too familiar today: The parents are divorced, and the beautiful story that began with young love ends tragically for all. It may have happened to your family or to the families of friends of yours. The hard fact is that today one out of two marriages fail.

Kids from broken homes keep asking themselves, sometimes all through their lives, "Why did this love of our parents for each other and us kids have to end this way?" Confused and angry, they cry out to their parents in the privacy of their feelings, "Don't tell us who have been hurt as deeply as you that we have no right to demand answers from you, no matter how personal, that make sense so that we, too, may understand what has happened. Otherwise, we shall be tormented and haunted all our lives by a tragedy you never helped us to comprehend and for which we may forever feel guilty, thinking that it may somehow have been our fault."

But life goes on, and divorced parents find new mates or never marry again. The kids get stepparents or foster parents or live in institutions or group homes. Still, for each one the tantalizing search goes on for that beautiful love story they all once knew. Only now it is harder to find, may not be the same, and if found, is harder to believe in.

No matter what has happened to your parents since those young days, it is important that you reach back in time and touch, as best you can, that love they had for each other. Have them tell you their story before it is lost forever. Have them dig out their early photographs, poems, and love letters to share with you so that you will understand and always remember.

Perhaps your parents were not among those who fell under the spell of romantic love. In modern generations, many young men and women resist the lure of burgeoning sexuality in favor of carving out careers for themselves and establishing secure life-styles before thinking about marriage and children. Such couples have an opportunity to develop their own personalities and thus bring an established body of values, beliefs, and interests to match with those of a possible lifetime mate.

In either case, children are best served by parents who not only sincerely love each other but also dearly love their children and are unequivocally dedicated to their welfare.

Suggested Questions for Discussion

1. How old were your parents when they fell in love?
2. Where and how did they meet?
3. Was it love at first sight or did it take some time before they came to love each other?
4. What attracted them to each other?
5. What are some of their special memories of those days?
6. Did their love have to face any difficult problems? How were they resolved?
7. How did their own parents feel about their being in love?
8. How much, if any, has their love changed with the years?
9. If your parents are divorced, do they still have warm feelings about those early days when they were in love?
10. What are your feelings about what your parents have told you?
11. Have your discussions with your parents helped you to understand them better? If not, why not?

CHAPTER II

To Love Is to Live Together

Two persons very much in love want very much to live together. They no longer want to spend just a few minutes or hours alone together. They want to be with each other all the time. They want to talk, eat, work, cry, laugh, sleep, and make love together as millions of lovers all over the world have done for thousands of years and will go on doing as long as there are human beings on earth.

But such a decision by two lovers can be of great concern to their parents. Parents conjure up all kinds of problems as they see their young son or daughter leave home to live with someone else. If it is a daughter, parents worry that she might become pregnant right away and that this might hurt her chances as a woman with other ambitions in life than just being a mother. For a son, the concern is his taking on the heavy responsibility of becoming a father so early in life and that this burden could ruin his chances of achieving a successful business or professional career.

Parents can also be apprehensive about any family differences that may exist between a young couple, such as religious beliefs and church affiliations, family background, ethnic origin, education, political convictions, and economic status.

If any of these deep-rooted and potentially explosive family differences exist, they can cause havoc if they require of each a strict adherence to family traditions.

That is why parents believe that the fewer there are of these highly sensitive family differences between young people who plan to live together, the better are their chances for a happy, stable life. Thus they prefer that their daughter or son marry

4

someone with beliefs and family background similar to their own.

Such agreeable conformity, however, is not usual for young couples because of the great diversity of beliefs among American families. Compromises or some kind of accommodation are often required if they hope to get along. Such compromises, experience shows, are not easily arrived at, and even if made they can leave a residue of bad feelings that may never be wholly dissipated. Sometimes all it requires is a seemingly slight irritation for the rankling feelings to erupt into a deluge of abusive language.

Perhaps you have seen that happen in your own family or with relatives when couples get angry and begin to call names or make slurs about each other's family background, religion, or politics.

Young couples in love, who are mostly involved in themselves, are unlikely to pay much attention to any family differences that may exist between them. More often than not they brush them aside as nuisances to be ignored. But in the ensuing years of living together the differences can reappear and cause real trouble. This is especially likely when they become parents and have to decide how the children are to be brought up, what they should believe, and what school or church they should attend.

If the necessary compromises are too numerous or of such a serious nature that they cannot be successfully negotiated, separation or divorce can follow. Family beliefs to some couples can mean more than their love for each other.

Some couples, however, will not allow family differences to threaten their love, no matter how sacred the differences may be to their respective families. To them, their love always comes first. Such couples may not have the security or stability that conformity to family beliefs may offer, but neither do they have the restrictions of conformity preventing them from experiencing and appreciating all the varied and rich choices that life has to offer. Moreover, they have the personal satisfaction of freely making their own decisions unhampered by family bias or prejudice.

What may be much more difficult for such couples to do is to give up strongly held viewpoints that each has developed, frequently in opposition to those held by his or her family. Because these views are so preciously one's own, they may be nonnegotiable and may endure tenaciously as a source of long-term feuding.

As for the style of living together, a popular arrangement for some couples is to live together unmarried. It is seen as an easy way out should a relationship falter or fail. Such a life-style shies away from a permanent commitment to one person.

Choosing this arrangement is not an uncommon reaction of young people to marriages they have known, maybe those of their own parents, whose outward appearance of love and tranquility was false. It is an expression of their disdain for husbands and wives who stay together, no matter how mutually destructive it may be, just for appearance's sake, for the so-called good of the children—which it never is—and to avoid "disgrace" to the family.

Because of the tentative and experimental nature of living together unmarried to see if it works, and if it doesn't so what, this life-style tends to undermine any strong desire to see that it does work. Also, the assumption that two persons in love cannot be hurt if the arrangement fails shows little understanding of the sensitivity of human feelings; it trivializes emotional attachments and makes a travesty of the depth, sincerity, and dynamics of human love.

Marriage, of course, remains more socially acceptable. Because of the ease of divorce, however, it is not notable as a commitment that assures the permanence and success of a relationship. Nor is the practice of trying to assure marital success by signing an agreement, like a labor-management contract, to do certain jobs and carry out specific responsibilities. Love, if it exists at all, needs no written contract or legal document to guarantee its success, only a primary commitment to see that it always comes before anything that might stand in its way or threaten its existence.

Suggested Questions for Discussion

1. Did your parents live together married or unmarried? How did they make the choice they did?
2. Were they happy with their choice? In retrospect would they decide differently? Why?
3. If they were married, when, where, and by whom?
4. Where did they live at first and what work did they do?
5. What was their life like when they began to live together?
6. What were the family backgrounds and beliefs that had a significant influence on their lives? Were they a cause for conflict between them?
7. If it was necessary, were your parents willing to work out their family differences? How was this accomplished and with what degree of success?
8. What personal convictions and beliefs did each of your parents develop, apart from those of their families, that meant much to them? Did they make for conflicts between them? How were they resolved?
9. Did your parents believe from the very beginning that their love for each other should always be first and allow nothing to come between them? Do they still believe that today?

CHAPTER III

Learning to Love and Live Together

If you were to ask your parents, they would probably tell you that it was not until they began to live together that they really came to know each other.

It is then that lovers learn that even though they agree on most controversial social, political, and religious issues, they still can have strong disagreements because of their different personalities. They learn that each has his or her own individual traits and behaviors, some of which may have great charm and appeal while others may not be so pleasant or easy to cope with.

It is only after people have lived together for some time and faced the frustrations of daily living that they begin to display some of the less attractive sides of their personality.

Depending on their early childhood experiences, how they were brought up, and the kind of parents they had, each lover brings to their living together certain behaviors associated with the past. Since no one is brought up perfectly, neither one of the couple will be without some unpleasant personal traits. Among the many possibilities, either one can be loving or cruel, cooperative or self-centered, irascible or kind, honest or deceitful, dependable or untrustworthy. What is important is to what degree the negative behaviors threaten a couple's love and trust.

Two persons in love can and do make many allowances (some even to the point of martyrdom) for each other's bad behavior just because they do love each other. But such tolerance can be stretched only so far, even for the most patient and forgiving lover. If love is to grow or even keep its

8

strength, it requires the continual nourishment of joy and warmth and kindness. If the negative behaviors become more numerous and frequent than the positive, the chances are that the relationship will fall apart. That can happen even early in a couple's life together.

Some behaviors are of such deep-rooted unresolved pathology arising from unfortunate early childhood experiences that no amount of love or tolerance can cure them. Only psychiatric care may be of any help.

As your parents know, and you must have observed yourself, many of the difficult behaviors of parents can be related to problems outside the home. Trying to make a living, disliking a job, being squeezed by a failing economy, being unable to complete one's education or job training, losing a job, are all emotionally upsetting factors that can result in bitter arguments and disenchantment between persons who love each other.

If persons in love do not recognize early enough what is happening to their relationship or are unwilling to act soon enough to solve or diminish their personality conflicts, psychological counseling may be the last hope to prevent a separation.

Nothing is sadder than the mental crippling of children of parents who have failed to resolve their serious interpersonal conflicts. These children can be damaged for life and as adults be unable to be good parents.

The problem of personality differences continues into adulthood and old age. With the changing of the years there are also changes in behavior. Such changes, however, should be no serious threat to those who love each other and who recognize and know how to handle destructive behavior when they see its early signs.

Living together may not always be easy. But to continue loving each other can make it not only easier but also very special and beautiful.

Suggested Questions for Discussion

1. What were the personality differences between your parents when they first lived together?
2. Were they a source of admiration? Of irritation and serious dispute?
3. If your parents had any serious personality differences, how did they resolve them?
4. Did differences result in separation and divorce?
5. Now that your parents can look back, were there any warning signs that they should have heeded to prevent confrontation over their differences?
6. Do they still have personal differences today? Are they serious? How do they handle them?

CHAPTER IV

Why Have a Baby?

When a young couple decide to live together, married or unmarried, they may not think of becoming parents right away. When they have moved into their apartment, home, or trailer, they are more likely at first to want to enjoy just being alone together before taking on the heavy job of having children.

It may also be that they cannot afford to have children while they are both working hard to earn a living. Or one of them may still be completing his or her education while the other earns their living.

Some couples feel that they need to postpone having children until they are well established in their profession or in the business world. That could mean that they would not become parents until they were in their 30's or 40's. Another restraint to early childbearing is the feeling of some couples that having children would affect their love for each other, that it would have to be shared with another. Then there are those who do not want children at all because they value their freedom more than parenthood with all its burdens and responsibilities.

"Why, then," you may ask, "does a couple want to have a baby?"

If you were to ask this of friends and relatives who have children, and of your parents, you would probably get a variety of answers. Husbands and wives might also differ in their opinions. All, however, would express a strong love of children—arising from the basic biological roles of man and woman, whose bodies are specifically equipped to attract each

11

other to make babies and whose maternal and paternal feelings are to feed, cuddle, protect, and enjoy their offspring as
other mammals do.

But with the human mammal it is not quite that simple.
Upon the biological base shared by other mammals, human
parents and human society have constructed a highly complex
structure of dreams, hopes, and social goals for the human
child. Many of those can be self-serving; that is, the birth of a
child may be looked upon primarily according to how it may
or may not serve the welfare of the parents and the society
into which it is born.

In countries such as India and China where the birthrates
are high and there is insufficient food to feed the large popula-
tions, the official public policy is to control population
through rigid birth-control practices. Other countries, which
need more human beings for military defense or for a large
work force, encourage and even give special recognition to
parents who produce large families. Having many children as
helping hands was traditionally a practice among the farm
families of earlier America.

Large families have also served as a convenient resource for
spreading religious beliefs, political doctrines, and family line-
age and as a cheap pool of labor for industry. It was not too
many years ago that the United States had to pass labor laws
to prevent the exploitation of young children, forced to work
long hours at hard labor in the coal mines and factories under
inhumane and brutal conditions.

It is an understandable inducement for human beings to
propagate their own kind that they are given in turn something of themselves, outside of themselves but part of their
own flesh and blood—a child—to serve as a reflection of
themselves. Perhaps the child will serve almost as a clone to
admire and love as one might admire and love one's self in a
mirror. But the paradox is this: Parents can and yet cannot

see themselves in their child as in a mirror. It sometimes takes someone else—a friend, a teacher, a psychologist, or even their own child—to show parents what they have not seen all along: a son or daughter who has his or her own distinct identity and needs to be appreciated, respected, and loved for that very fact.

Some couples have such strong maternal and paternal feelings that they will go to any lengths to adopt a baby if they are unable to have a child of their own. Others are ready to place a mother's life at risk, if need be, to achieve that end. Some even raise a whole family of adopted children.

Not all women feel that way about having a baby. Some are terrified by the thought. They fear the dangers of childbirth, worry about looking ugly while pregnant, and have no confidence that they will be a good mother. Then that awful fear lurks in their minds of the possibility of giving birth to a physically or mentally handicapped child.

But the tremendous joy and satisfaction a woman experiences in having a baby of her own who has lived and grown within her body for nine months more than makes up for any of the real or imagined suffering she may have had to endure.

Fathers also can have their concerns. They may worry that a baby will estrange them from their wife because of the care and attention a newborn child will demand of its mother. Some fathers even feel resentful and jealous of the baby until they themselves become physically involved in caring for it. Fathers also have understandable concerns about the long-term financial commitment required in raising a child, especially if there are already other children whose care is painfully stretching the family's pocketbook.

But given all the reasons that a couple may have for wanting a baby, the big question remains whether their own relationship is sound enough to offer a child an optimum environment in which to grow. If not, is it right to have a baby? Unfortunately, there are parents who do not think of the welfare of the baby in making that decision.

It can only be a terrible disservice to a child and a cruel hoax for a couple to believe that the remedy for serious marital conflict is to have a baby to patch things up. Couples who subscribe to this quick-fix solution for their interpersonal problems can end up with a quick-fix divorce by the time the baby is born.

Not all babies are conceived purposely or by plan. Some are conceived by "accident," meaning that the partners were not careful enough with birth-control methods. That does not mean that the parents will have less love for a child who was thus conceived. Sometimes such lack of prevention can mask an underlying desire by one or both parents to have a baby, if only by "accident." To guarantee a greater degree of protection, especially if the parents already have children and do not want any more, the wife may decide to be sterilized or the father to have a vasectomy.

Parents who do little if any planning for parenthood can end up having so many children that they are unable financially to take care of any new additions to the family. For the good of the baby, they put it up for adoption with the hope that some couple may provide a better life than they can for their child.

Some pregnant women have an abortion to avoid having a baby. This can happen as a result of not wanting a baby, or being too poor to support a baby, or being too ill to bear a baby. Whatever the reason, the practice of abortion has involved heated debate about the morality of destroying the life of the fetus in the uterus.

The moral issue of protecting the life of the human fetus loses much of its persuasion when it overlooks the thousands of born babies who are as much as aborted everyday by parental neglect, poverty, abuse, brutality, and the cold indifference to their plight of an affluent society.

Suggested Questions for Discussion

1. Did your parents want a baby soon after they began to live together?

2. What were their plans, if any, for having children?

3. Did they use birth-control methods?

4. Did your mother ever have a miscarriage?

5. What were the circumstances of your parents at the time of your conception?

6. Did your parents plan for your birth, or were you a happy "accident"?

7. Did your parents want a boy or a girl? Why?

8. Did your mother take any special training classes in preparation for your birth? Was your father involved?

CHAPTER V

How Does a Parent Learn to be a Parent?

Anyone knows that it is easier to have a baby than to raise one. That is particularly true of parents who have had no training or experience in the skills required in caring for an infant.

But where could parents have gained those skills even if they had wanted them?

Not likely in the modern home. Today the home is no longer the training center for young women whose role it is to stay at home and learn from mothers and grandmothers how to raise children.

Neither are today's schools of any help. They train and educate for almost everything but parenthood. How to be a good mother or father is not a course likely to be found in the curricula of our high schools or colleges. It is not considered one of the "basics," nor is it mentioned among the electives such as art, music, and drama. It is just not "creative" enough.

While persons in professions, businesses, or other occupations are required to have educational credentials, pass qualifying exams, and be legally licensed, just about anybody can be a parent with no training or experience or credentials at all. Far more value is placed on Mom and Dad for being tops in their business or profession than for being tops as parents. Where are the diplomas and degrees and medals for a good job done as parents?

It should come as no surprise, then, that parents who lack child-care skills have a hard time with their first baby. What is worse, a first baby is at the mercy of these untrained parents. The baby becomes something for the inexperienced parent to practice on and, perchance, by trial and error, learn how to do the right thing. A new family automobile can receive fairer treatment than that.

When a young mother does not know how to handle her first baby, she often invites her mother or mother-in-law to step in as a professed expert and demonstrate how the job should be done. As sincere as these offers of help may be, they can only add to a young mother's feeling of inadequacy. The presence of her own mother at her elbow telling her what to do with her baby wakens that old feeling of little-girl dependency, and any help from her mother-in-law she sees as confirmation to her husband of her own failure as a mother.

Fortunately, some prospective parents have enough sense to remedy their ignorance by taking courses on baby care given by professionals and sponsored by parent groups or public health agencies. Wisely, these parents-to-be also seek the guidance of a pediatrician before the baby is due.

Such study groups discuss not only the management of the physical needs and health of the baby—feeding, bathing, clothing, periodic medical checkups—but also the psychological care of the baby, its stages of development, sensitivity to its behavioral needs, and awareness of the parents' own feelings toward the baby. Do they feel at ease or uncomfortable with the baby? Do they feel free in expressing their affection for the baby, or do they hold back their feelings? Are they easily upset if the baby cries, or do they remain patient and understanding? Are they proud or embarrassed about how the baby looks? Would they rather have had a boy than a girl? Or a girl rather than a boy? More to the point, do or don't they love their baby and accept it as it is?

It may seem strange to you as a young person to learn that there are parents who struggle with such problems.

Even with education and training, some parents still fail to agree on how to raise their baby. Their disagreements may stem from what each believes was the right or wrong way their parents raised them, or how soon they should institute parental authority so as to assure that they, not the baby, are in command.

They may also hold different goals for the child. The father of a boy may see him, even as an infant, as a superior athlete. The mother, on the other hand, may have quite different ambitions for the child. The cultural stereotyping and self-serving goals of the parents come into play, with each casting the child in a mold of his or her own dreams and hopes.

If the parents love and respect each other and are willing to make allowances for each other's personality differences, they should in all fairness do the same for the new member they have invited to join the family. Since no two babies have the same personalities, they deserve, as fellow humans, the acknowledgment of this fact by their parents. A significant step that some parents take in that direction is their early recognition that a baby is no mere replica of the parents nor a blueprint of what they would like it to be. But that is very hard for parents to do.

Customarily, parents see their role as the teacher of the baby, when in fact the baby has much to teach them as well—that is, if the parents have enough humility to allow themselves to be taught, to watch and listen to the important things it is trying to tell them about itself, about them, and its environment.

It is this reciprocal interchange at the very beginning of the parent-child relationship, this sharing of the dual role of teacher and pupil, that makes the child and the parents partners in the years they live together.

If, at any age of the child, this shared communication stops, so ends their partnership and with it the love and respect they have for each other. By now, in high school, you must be well acquainted with this fact, from your own experiences or from those of your own age.

Unfortunately, far too many babies have parents who never learn or even care to learn to be good parents, or who do so poorly as parents that their kids can say with self-punishing bitterness and anger, "I wish I never had parents" or "I wish I never was born."

Perhaps they are right, for these are kids whose happiness in life will always be at risk.

Suggested Questions for Discussion

1. How did your parents learn to be parents?

2. What was the life situation of your parents when you were a baby? Did both of them work? Who took care of you?

3. Did your parents know how to take care of you as a baby?

4. Did they have any problems with you as a baby? If so, what did they do?

5. What were some of the popular trends at the time in raising babies? Did your parents subscribe to any of them in taking care of you?

6. Were there any serious disagreements between your parents on how to raise you? If so, how were they resolved?

7. Did you as a baby bring your parents closer together, or were you the cause of estrangement between them?

8. Did your parents easily and freely give you love and affection, or were they reserved about expressing their love for you?

9. Do your parents think it was better that you were or were not their first child? Why?

10. What were some of the hopes and dreams your parents had for you as a baby? Do they still have the same hopes and dreams for you today? Are they different from the ones you now have for yourself?

11. As your parents look back to those days when you were an infant, do they think they did the best they could for you? Would they have done anything differently?

CHAPTER VI

Raising Kids

At this time in your life when you are in high school and some years away from infancy, it would be interesting to see how well you can identify the kind of training you received from your parents that you believe determined the special person you are today. It would also be worthwhile for you to find out from your parents how they justified raising you the way they did, for there are as many ways of raising kids as there are beliefs on how to accomplish that task.

Although there appears to be some movement away from the role of parents as the supreme master in the home, far too many of the decisions and decision-making processes that affect kids of your age are still made by parents without the participation of their kids. Too frequently all that kids get from parents are interdictions against doing this or thinking that. Implied is the assumption by parents that kids would rather do and think things against their best interests because they just don't care or know any better. That, of course, may well be true of kids who were never given the responsibility to learn to think and act for themselves.

The cornerstone of the autocracy of some parents seems to be their conviction that they alone know what is best for their kids—the right religion, the right ideas, the right political beliefs, the right books, the right friends, the right wars. The history of parents who have always set the directions for mankind hardly demonstrates such flawless wisdom.

The parent assumes the role of a supersalesperson, with the kid an unwitting consumer not free to explore a variety of attractive items before making a purchase, but a consumer incarcerated in the home where there is but one item on the shelf to buy—that offered by the parent. Such parents believe that what they have to sell is the best item of its kind and that any kid in his or her right mind would be lucky to be given the opportunity to covet it.

The main transgression that some parents fail to recognize is as important to kids as taxation without representation was to the founding fathers who laid down their lives over it. If kids rebel against the autocracy of parents, it is because they are never given the chance to question parental fiats or to be invited as partners to join in deciding matters that affect their lives. As a result, these kids grow up unable to make wise decisions for themselves.

Underlying this negative approach to the thinking ability of kids is lack of respect for the young brain of the human species with its inherent ability and hunger to explore, experience, evaluate, and understand everything—to open doors to the world, not shut them tight, as some parents do to kids.

It is this restrictive policy that severely handicaps the ability of kids to cope with the world about them. There is no more pervasive and dogged activity of human beings than their determination to seduce and persuade their fellows, by whatever means, to believe and do as they do, whether in politics, religion, education, life-style, or the purchase of soap powder. As never before, the seductive and persistent persuasiveness of the communication media is threatening the questioning mind with overwhelming power.

Thus, it becomes more important than ever for kids to know how to make their own considered judgments so as to be able to cope with a rapidly developing mind-controlling technology.

Because it is also a time in the history of man when the traditional distinctions between young and old are rapidly being obliterated with the prospects of worldwide devastation by nuclear war, kids must now look to themselves, no longer to their parents and other adults, to protect their welfare. How can they rely on the traditional wisdom and guidance of the adult world when it offers them nothing but total annihilation as a choice for their future?

Suggested Questions for Discussion

1. How have your parents raised you? Ask them for explanations of why they raised you as they did.
2. Did they follow any special educational theories or viewpoints in raising you?
3. Did they encourage you to develop skills to think and act independently? Do they practice such skills themselves?
4. Do your parents include you in the decision-making of the family?
5. Are your parents satisfied with the way they raised you? Why?
6. Did your parents have any problems that made it hard for them to raise you the way they would have liked?
7. Do you think they did a good job in raising you? If not, how would you have liked them to have raised you differently?

CHAPTER VII

Parents of the Handicapped

It is often said, and with considerable supporting evidence, that the greatest challenge to any parent is to raise a handicapped child.

Defined as some disadvantage or shortcoming, the word "handicapped" can encompass just about everyone, for no one is without some handicap or other in functioning adequately in the daily affairs of human life.

There is the student who is poor in reading, math, or foreign language who needs special tutoring to overcome his or her weakness. There is the shy boy who may need dancing lessons to overcome his timidity with girls. Those in poor physical condition may require a strict regimen of diet and exercise. A parent with marital problems may need counseling. The list of human inadequacies and disadvantages can include all kinds of persons from parents to kids to the President of the United States.

The part of the handicapped population that concerns parents the most, however, is the physically disadvantaged, the mentally retarded, and the emotionally disabled. The degree of their concern is related to the degree of severity and complexity of the handicap. They also worry about the stigma and penalties that society places on certain handicaps in its hierarchy of socially acceptable and unacceptable deficiencies.

It is one thing to be physically disadvantaged and in a wheelchair, but if you also drool because your mouth muscles cannot control the flow of saliva, that is something else. It is also something else if you have a good mind but can only grunt and groan when you try to speak. Or if you are fifteen and have no visible handicaps but think and speak like a four-year-old. Equally unacceptable are the emotionally disabled, many of whom live in a fantasy world unrelated to the events and people around them.

The stigma and penalties suffered by the handicapped increase in proportion to their mental incapacities, for the measure of success and acceptability in a competitive society such as ours is closely related to possessing a capable brain. What can an incompetent brain have to offer society that is of any value? That is why more money is poured into curing or replacing bad hearts, bad kidneys, bad livers, or just about any other organ of the body but a bad brain.

Because the mentally retarded are at the bottom rung of the ladder of success, they are the least useful to society. They become the discards that cannot be discarded. Hitler in World War II solved the problem by consigning all the mentally retarded to crematoriums. We, professedly more humane, pile them into inadequate, understaffed, underfinanced, crowded state and county institutions or into makeshift community group homes that are equally ill equipped to meet their needs.

Given this picture of society's neglect and rejection of the mentally handicapped, it is understandable that one of the first things a new mother does is to take her baby in her arms and carefully examine every inch of its body to be sure it is not handicapped.

Should it turn out that the child is mentally handicapped, the parents must face the social ostracism of the child and the impact that can have on their own lives. Parents who have never had a mentally retarded child cannot conceive how difficult, costly, and lonely this long journey can be.

In trying to save parents from such a lifelong burden, which can bring mental breakdown and divorce to their lives, some doctors urge that the mentally retarded infant be institutionalized immediately before the parents become too attached to it and unable to part with it.

If the parents decide to keep the baby at home, they will soon find out that few doctors and clinics know enough about that kind of child to be able to help in its care and training. Medical schools have always been remiss in training doctors in this area. Parents will also find that early childhood training centers are few and difficult to find. Those that do exist are usually started and run by the toil and tears of parents who have such kids.

When the child reaches school age, the parents will discover that many public schools do not have classes or programs for the mentally handicapped. The few special education classes in the public school system have the status of compounds for unwanted second-class children: barely tolerated, crowded, staffed with poorly trained teachers or untrained volunteers, having a miserable budget and hand-me-down educational equipment. Where any special education does exist for these kids, it is often no more than a token baby-sitting service; the schools, as a part of a social system that values only high-achieving kids, would rather not put their money on the non-achievers. It is not a good investment. It is not money well spent.

If the mentally retarded boy or girl is of your age, he or she will face the jeers, prejudices, and discrimination so common toward these kids. You have probably seen it happen in your school. Friends for these kids are hard to find and harder to keep when found. How many so-called normal kids you know would have the courage to have a mentally retarded kid for a friend? What social penalties would he or she be willing to pay to keep such a friendship?

To avoid social disgrace and embarrassment, some parents keep retarded children in the house and never allow them out in the community. Some even lock them in attics so that not even their friends know they have a mentally retarded child.

Those who take the child outside are beset by guilt for making people feel uncomfortable by imposing on them the bizarre or inappropriate behavior of their handicapped child. If the child also has distorted features, the parents suffer additional distress in a society that places a high premium on pretty faces and good looks.

The emotional toll on these parents can be cruel and ruthless. Out of their frustration and anger toward a society that shows them no pity or support, they turn their wrath on each other and even take out their deep personal hurt on their handicapped child, only to shed bitter tears of anguish and regret for having done so.

What happens to these kids when the parents are too old to care for them? What happens to them when they are adults and the parents are no longer living to help them?

There are always the state institutions for the mentally retarded if they are not too crowded; or the jails, whose population is largely made up of the mentally defective who so easily can get in trouble with the law; or the city streets, where they can be seen during the day scavenging in garbage cans for scraps of food and at night sleeping in dark hallways and alleys curled up in old newspapers to keep warm.

Finally, for many of them, all that is left is the city morgue.

Suggested Questions for Discussion

1. Do your parents have any handicaps? If so, what are they?

2. How serious are they?

3. Do they freely acknowledge them, or are they sensitive and secretive about them?

4. Do these handicaps affect their relationship? If so, how?

5. What, if anything, have they done to cope with their handicaps?

6. Do you have any handicaps that make it difficult for you to function physically, socially, emotionally, or academically? If so, what are they?

7. Do your parents recognize and acknowledge any handicaps you may have?

8. How do you view any handicaps you may have? Do your parents agree with your viewpoint, or is there a difference of opinion? Why?

9. Are your parents ashamed or embarrased about any handicaps you may have? How do you know how they feel?

10. Do your parents blame each other for any handicaps you may have? What do they say? What do you feel about what they say?

11. What, if anything, has been or is being done to help you with any handicaps you may have?

12. If you have any handicaps, do you think your parents are helpful and supportive of your efforts to cope with them?

CHAPTER VIII

Schooling

If there is anything that makes for bitter debate, fury, and total alienation between kids and parents, it is schooling. Since kids spend most of their lives in school, parents and society expect them to excel in their studies. If they do not, they are in trouble.

What counts on report cards are the A's and B's. Common-as-dirt C's and stupid D's are never acceptable even for such subjects as cooking and chorus. If an array of F's decorates the report card, a brigade of school psychologists flanked by columns of counselors is marched out to deal with the culprit.

It is only then, perhaps for the first time, that some parents become involved in their kids. More likely than not it is the mother, not the father, who visits the principal's office for consultation about their problem kid.

To some fathers, what happens to their kid at school is not their job but the mother's, as it is the mothers, not the fathers, who are expected to take the kids to the doctor when they are sick. It is only when kids are old enough to leave high school and must decide on their future that some dads think it is their turn to enter the act and take over as the experts in such weighty matters of the world.

It may be hard to conceive, but some parents do not know, or even care, where their kids go to school. Or if they do, they have not the slightest idea who their kids' teachers are or where their classrooms are; they are unable to say what subjects their kids are being taught and haven't the faintest notion of the teaching methods used in the school.

Nor do they ever attend a PTA meeting to find out. PTA

meetings are notorious for their poor attendance by parents. In some schools only a handful of parents (usually the same old bunch) turn up for meetings, huddled together in the front row of a large empty school auditorium. On stage there are more teachers than there are parents in the auditorium.

A good test of your own parents' interest in your education is to compare the amount of time they give to your schooling to the amount of time they spend in pursuing their hobbies and other activities.

Too often when a kid has a learning problem at school, the response of the parent is, "If you worked harder you'd get it," rather than taking time to search out with the kid and the school the possible causes of the problem.

How many parents make it a practice, as they do with doctor and dentist appointments, to make periodic visits to school whether or not their kid has a problem? By doing so, any early evidence of a possible difficulty can be handled by prompt diagnosis and treatment. "Preventive education" is as important as preventive medicine.

Parents who are uninterested in their kids' schooling are likely to be equally indifferent to homework. If they show any interest at all, it is probably to see that the kids do the homework and not watch TV, so that the parents can see their favorite soap operas without interference.

Homework, as these parents remember it from their school days, is a bitter but necessary medicine that is supposed to toughen kids up to face the rough world outside. Since they see no more redeeming value to homework than that, they certainly have no desire to participate with their kids in a punishment that they feel they don't deserve at their age. They had enough of that stuff when they were kids.

It is these same indifferent parents who are likely to shout the loudest when their kid gets a poor report card. They will blame everyone but themselves. Of course, there is always the likely prospect that they will take it out on each other as well.

They will not only blame their kids for academic failure, but also vehemently take the school to task for not doing its job. If teachers did their jobs well, so they believe, kids would not get bad grades. After all, a good teacher, like a good mechanic with a car, should be able to keep a kid in top running order.

Fruitful learning for kids requires more fertile and nourishing soil than parents who do not care about their education and school systems that try to run thousands of overcrowded classrooms on bare-bones budgets with overworked and underpaid teachers.

The young human brain, with its inherent curiosity about everything in the world, needs no grades as an incentive to learn. There are kids whose hunger for learning is so great that they will not be put down by anything or anyone in their search to satisfy that hunger—not poor schools nor the neglect of parents. The joy of learning is their life. They must look, observe, explore, seek, study, and know everything, even poke around in dark and often forbidden corners to ask hard, sometimes threatening questions and to find new, disturbing answers.

Such kids are the bane of parents and teachers who do not like to be challenged. In homes and schools where unquestioning conformity to ideas and beliefs is the norm, these unruly brains can be understandably obnoxious.

"Whence comes this unorthodoxy?" parents and schools ask themselves, never suspecting that perhaps it was the parents indifference and the school's sterile, stifling rote learning that drove these young questioning minds to pursue learning as it should be pursued—with freedom, joy, and excitement.

Suggested Questions for Discussion

1. How interested are your parents in your schooling? How do they or do they not show their interest?

2. If they are not interested in your schooling, why do you think they are not?

3. Are your parents willing to help you with your homework? If not, why not?

4. Is your schooling a matter of considerable discussion at home? Have any of these discussions been helpful to you?

5. How much time do your parents give to keeping well informed about your schooling? Do you believe the time they give is enough?

6. Do you think your parents know what takes place in your school? In your classrooms? What subject matter is being taught and how?

7. How frequently do your parents visit school to meet with your teachers? Is there a good rapport between them? Do they know and respect each other?

8. Do your parents meet with your teachers only when there are problems, or do they make a point of being kept informed on your work and what, if anything, they and your teachers might do to help you?

9. Are you involved in these parent-teacher sessions about your work? If not, why not?

10. If you have attended such sessions, have they been helpful to you?

11. Do your parents attend all PTA meetings at your school? Do they participate in the discussions? Are they active in the organization?

12. How do you think your parents can help you most with your schooling?

CHAPTER IX

Playing Favorites

Kids at a very early age can tell when parents play favorites in the family. They know simply by the amount of love and attention bestowed on one child as compared to what the other children receive.

The practice is more than playing games with children, of having fun, as some parents would like you to believe. Unfortunately, it can result in serious long-term consequences for those who are not favored. The self-confidence that adults have or do not have depends largely on how favorably or unfavorably parents thought about them as children. Children who are victims of parental bias can be haunted through life by a crippling sense of personal inadequacy.

This dangerous game can begin as soon as a baby is born. Even as the parents are showing friends and relatives what a beautiful baby they have, they may already feel stirrings of prejudice and negative feelings toward the child. This can happen, for instance, if the parents wanted a boy and were disapointed when they got a girl, or if the baby happens to look like a relative whom they dislike. On the other hand, a feeling of favoritism may be engendered in the father if the baby, especially if it is a boy, looks like him.

Favoritism or lack of favoritism when kids are older can be influenced by what parents like or do not like about themselves. Seeing their own strengths and weaknesses reflected in their older kids, parents can react to them with admiration or displeasure.

Although it is not always easy or possible to understand why some parents give or withhold their love and attention, much insight might be gained by exploring with your parents what favoritism they experienced when they were kids. It could offer clues to their behavior if they do show favoritism among their kids today. It is not uncommon for favoritism that parents experienced as kids to be reflected in how they now feel about certain children in the family.

A firstborn child is often a favorite of parents simply because it is the first and, therefore, special. But parents often expect more of this child than it can possibly achieve. As the eldest in the family, for example, the first child is epected to be the perfect surrogate parent to the other kids, a model for them to emulate, be guided by, and even punished by if necessary. Such a heavy responsibility places an intolerable burden on this child.

Since it is often impossible for the favorite child to meet the high demands of the parents, she or he is, ironically, subject to the most criticism. It is a question whether firstborn kids, when adults, will successfully weather the damage done to them by the exacting demands of their parents. As adults, many of them are likely to punish themselves with the same high expectations because of the years spent as children in the demanding role thrust upon them by their parents.

Favoritism by parents may depend not only on such factors as whether a child is a boy or girl, whether a child has certain physical traits similar to those of the parents or is attractive or unattractive in appearance. As the child grows older, favoritism may depend on whether the child is a success or failure in school. If there is anything that a parent wants most, it is a child with brains who can do outstanding academic work. That is the kid who gets top grades in school, who obeys parents and never gets in trouble, and who is a sure winner of the parents' favor.

No such good fortune is in store for the unfavored kid because she or he does not quite fit into the parents' idea of a "good" kid. This kid becomes the "bad" kid in the family, not only to the parents, but also to the siblings who, taking their cue from the parents, pick on him or her as fair game. This favoritism by parents that the other kids imitate can only cause more rivalry, strengthen the pecking order, and create general bad feeling in the family.

This approach to the "bad" kid in the family makes him or her even worse. Rather than recognizing and admitting their own complicity in producing a "bad" kid, the parents place the full blame on the child.

Because these kids are not favored at the very time in their lives when they most need help and some special love and attention, rather than condemnation and rejection, they are unable to pull themselves through the period. They are stigmatized as incorrigibles at school, at home, and in society. They become prime candidates for long-term delinquency.

It is one thing to give special love and attention to a kid who is having a tough time growing up. It is quite another thing, however, for parents to play favorites with kids out of prejudice and personal preference. Such parents have yet to grow up themselves.

Suggested Questions for Discussion

1. Do your parents play favorites with their kids? If so, how?

2. Who are the favorites of your parents? Why do you think so?

3. If you are a favorite of your parents, why is that so and how do you feel about it?

4. If you are not a favorite, how do you feel about it? Why do you think you are not?

5. Do your parents differ in whom they favor in the family? Why?

6. If your parents do play favorites, do you ever let them know how you feel about it? What do they say?

7. Do you think there is ever a good reason for parents to favor a kid? What would it be?

8. If your parents play favorites, how do you think it affects the family?

CHAPTER X

The Communication Gap

If parents and kids could see the world the same way, there probably would be no problems between them, at least none serious enough to damage their relationship. That also holds true for the countries that make up the world family of nations.

But peace and goodwill are not the reality that always exists in the home or in the world. Yet if we demand, as we do, that the family of nations keep the lines of communication open to achieve mutual respect and to avoid conflict, does it make any sense to ask less of parents and kids who make up the world family of nations.

Parents see the world as their own experiences have taught them to see it from early childhood. The same is true of their kids, but they are seeing a world that is different from the world their parents knew. So what's new? That is a problem as old as human history. It is not just seeing the world differently that is the problem; it is how parents and kids can successfully mediate those differences.

Perhaps if parents and kids told each other how and why they view the world differently, they might get along better. Though they might not even then agree, they might at least have some understanding of why they disagree and learn how best to get along together despite their disagreements.

That, however, requires a level of communication that may not be readily available to them if parents have not made it a practice since their kids were little to talk openly and frequently with them. That means a dialogue, not a lecture.

If this nurturing verbal interchange is allowed to wither and die because parents are so wrapped up in their own interests

36

that they have no time for their kids, then parents and kids can lose, perhaps forever, the last lines of warm and friendly communication with each other. Once that is allowed to happen, parents and kids become strangers who no longer know each other and soon do not even care if they don't. Such estrangements can only invite more misunderstanding, bitter arguments, and acrimony that can drive parents and kids even further apart.

The situation is not the insurmountable generation gap that one hears so much about. Not unlike many other gaps in human relations, the so-called generation gap is basically a communication gap that all human beings experience, no matter who they are or what their age or relationship, when they have misunderstandings or fallings out.

The fact is that the world is full of communication gaps that everyone has to bridge every day with all kinds and ages of human beings if one is to get along in life. Thus, parents and kids have no monopoly on the problem. Like all the rest of humanity, they too must learn to bridge the gap.

It is especially important for them to do, since verbal communication is one of the basic means for human beings to express their love for each other. The great literature of the world attests to that. So also does the vernacular heard every day. When there is love and respect, people speak with love and respect to each other, without the need of sophisticated language. They can even do so quite well with slang.

At first it is by the physical contact of cuddling, hugging, caressing, and kissing that parents express their love for a baby. But as kids grow older these physical expressions of love between parents and kids are often disguised in the subtleties of language.

By the time the kids are grown up they find it uncomfortable (thanks to our restrictive mores) to say freely, "I love you, Dad" or "I love you, Mom." Now it must be done more by implication, conveyed in the tone and feeling expressed. (It is interesting that parents and kids are more forthright with their language of anger than with their expressions of love for each other.)

Even in the most mundane conversations between kids and parents, one can tell whether there is affection and respect for each other. This is true of any dialogue whether between husbands and wives, teachers and students, or heads of nations.

If you want to know how much members of a family mean to each other, listen to how they talk to each other. A useful diagnostic device would be a conversation barometer to register the emotional climate between members of a family as they talk with each other.

If the prevailing emotional weather is stormy, with angry thunder and lightning rolling through the house most of the day and night, it can only make kids and parents want to avoid and finally escape from each other for their own peace of mind. Actually, kids do just that—they run away. Parents separate and divorce.

It is sad to see kids your age have such poor communication with their parents. Too often one hears kids say that it is easier and more worthwhile to talk to other adults, even strangers, than to their own parents. It is especially sad because if the doors of friendly and warm dialogue are once shut between parents and kids, they may never be opened again. That is why it is crucial to keep the dialogue alive between parents and kids, who should always love each other no matter how differently they see the world.

The commitment to communication is one that all human beings must make if we are to keep our homes and the world places of love, not hate.

Suggested Questions for Discussion

1. How well do you and your parents communicate with each other?

2. Is it easier for you to talk with your parents now than when you were younger?

3. Do you enjoy talking with your parents? Why or why not?

4. Do you have frequent talks together? If not, do you think you should?

5. Do you ever have good heart-to-heart talks? If not, would you like to?

6. Who is more likely to initiate a dialogue?

7. Do you have talks mostly with one parent and not the other?

8. Which parent is it easier for you to talk with? Why?

9. What do you mostly talk about with your parents? Are the topics you discuss usually limited and the same?

10. Who does most of the talking when you have a conversation with your parents?

11. Do your parents mostly lecture you rather than talk with you?

12. What do you mostly agree or not agree on?

13. How do you reconcile your differences, if at all?

14. Are you satisfied with the way differences are resolved?

15. Are there topics you believe it best not to discuss with your parents? Why or why not?

16. What subjects are the most difficult to discuss with your parents?

17. What topics are the easiest to discuss?

18. Do you and your parents keep in control while discussing your differences?

19. As you discuss your differences, are you aware of how you speak to each other, the tone of voice, the choice of language?

20. Do you and your parents come away from your talks together feeling good? Frustrated? Dissatisfied?

CHAPTER XI

Parent Panic Over Adolesents

Characteristically parents have always shown great concern for their kids when they reach adolescence, a period roughly from thirteen to eighteen years of age—the so-called teens. The concern arises from the uncertainty parents feel when kids go through the transition from dependence on parents to a growing freedom and independence as they approach adulthood.

Because of the deep emotional ties that parents develop with children over many years, it is not easy to allow them during adolescence to begin to make their own decisions.

Some parents find it so nearly impossible that, instead of loosening their hold on maturing kids, they come down harder on them with prohibitions that allow very little room for independent thought. As a result the kids remain like the little children they were. They become what is often derisively known as a "Mamma's boy" or a "Daddy's girl." When they grow up they find it hard to behave like independent and self-assured adults. If they marry, they continue to be like children to their husbands and wives and even to their own children, some of whom may act more adult than they do.

Parents who deny kids the opportunity to develop the skills required to be a competent adult may spare themselves what they see as the trauma of having rebellious adolescents on their hands, but they do so only at a great price to their kids, who are likely to pay for this parental bondage for the rest of their lives.

Whether kids will be rebellious or cooperative during adolescence depends on how their parents raised them from child-hood. Kids who were given the opportunity at an early age to evaluate choices and make their own decisions are more likely to make the transition to adulthood with comparative ease and success. They will also have a background of experience that will prove indispensable to them as adults.

Kids who have been allowed to think and act for themselves have little to rebel against that should cause parents to panic. Rebellious kids are more likely to be those who were never allowed to think for themselves or given their right to face the facts and hard choices they must make in arriving at intelligent decisions. These kids now feel forced to fight with their parents who have taken this right away from them. As they near adulthood they feel impelled to make a strong protest, even to rebel.

Kids who have learned to think for themselves are more prepared to handle the pressure of all the commercial hype and superficial values to which adolescents are constantly subject. They are also well equipped to take in stride anything with which the world might like to bend their minds when they are full-fledged adults.

Even kids who have learned early to stand on their own feet always feel a touch of sorrow when they must take leave of youth and enter adult life. At first it may seem of little consequence to them to part with parents as the grownup world beckons them on. Only later, when they too are parents and their children take leave of them, will they fully understand and appreciate this important step in their life, especially if they have had parents who helped them to think for themselves.

Parents always feel the pain and loss of this separation from their kids, but there will be pride, too, if they have done their job well. They will be satisfied that their kids are capable of carrying on their lives long after the parents have gone.

Suggested Questions for Discussion

1. How do you think your parents view adolescent kids?
2. Why do you think parents are so frequently concerned about adolescent kids?
3. If they have any concerns, do you think they are justified?
4. Do your parents view this period in your life the same way you do? If there are differences, what are they? Why?
5. If there are differences, how do you resolve them, if you do?
6. Have your parents always urged and helped you to make your own decisions? If not, why not?
7. Do your parents now allow you more freedom to think and act on your own? If not, why not?

CHAPTER XII

Are Mothers and Fathers Different?

Almost everyone has a sense that there is a difference between mothers and fathers, but no one is quite sure how to define it. If pressed to explain the difference, most people would probably fall back on the differing personalities of their own parents. The question arises as to how much the personality of each parent is due to such environmental factors as the social customs, traditional roles, and family upbringing that mold boys and girls, men and women, fathers and mothers, to fit into what society wants them to be. The function and place of mothers and fathers change in society as their traditional roles change, as we see so well demonstrated in today's parents.

If parents were stripped of all the trappings and role expectations that society places on them, would there be any basic differences between them?

The biological reality is that it is the mother who carries the baby in her body, not the father, who only helps conceive it when it is an egg in the mother's uterus. For nine months the baby is nurtured by the mother inside the mother. And when the baby is born, it is the mother, not the father, who feeds the baby with her own milk. It is the mother, not the father, who for the most part takes care of the baby long after it is born.

Because of this basic biological role of the mother, she has a special place in the minds and feelings of everyone. The very name "mother" in any language rings a wholly different set of bells than does the name "father." Whether we consciously remember them or not when older, the sensory pleasures of nursing, touching, and caressing experienced between mother and child are deeply implanted in the mind of every person. It is our baby experiences that make it possible for us to know how to love others.

The father, because he is not as biologically and sensorily associated with the newborn as the mother is, has at first a somewhat ambiguous role to play with the infant. Initially, the baby expresses this fact by seeing the father as a stranger who causes him to cry and whom he rejects out of jealousy for taking away the attention of the mother. By slow stages, however, the baby finally accepts the father as a friend and as an important member of a love triangle that is bonded together by the feelings of love and tenderness the parents have for each other.

In previous generations the biological differences between the parents during the childbearing and child-rearing years dictated the traditional roles of mother and father in society. Today that has all changed. Whereas only a few years ago a mother's place was in the home taking care of the children and the father's was out in the world working to support the family, today many mothers are employed outside the home and more and more are pursuing full-time careers. Whereas once the family was a close-knit, interdependent unit, today it is in disarray, if not in shambles, because of broken homes, separation, divorce, single parents living with kids, complicated living arrangements between parents, and fluid love relationships among husbands, wives, and auxiliary lovers.

No longer do wives and husbands reflect their biological differences by their roles and responsibilities in the family, by their mental or physical abilities, or by their interest and performance in certain endeavors that once were the domain of one sex alone.

Even biological parenthood has changed radically. There is now the so-called surrogate mother who bears a child for a wife who is unable to do so herself. The fertilized egg of the wife is implanted in the womb of the surrogate mother, who brings it to term. There is the "test-tube" baby conceived outside the mother's body. The mother's egg is fertilized by the father's sperm in a laboratory and then implanted in the wife's uterus. This is done because the wife's egg is unable to reach the uterus to be fertilized by the husband's sperm. Then there is the conception of a baby by sperm from a sperm bank injected into the womb, usually that of a single woman who wishes to have a baby without having a husband. She receives the sperm of an unknown donor, a member of a group of brilliant men who have contributed their sperm to a special sperm bank so as to perpetuate their genes by creation of exceptionally intelligent children.

Probably the most radical of these changes in biological parenthood is the surrogate mother. It is too early to say what will be the significance of this method of motherhood in the relationship between the real mother and her child born of another woman. It is also too early to tell what will be the outcome for a child born of a single mother from the sperm of an unknown father.

One is tempted to ask, "Will a time come when it will be difficult to see any differences between husbands and wives, when the biological and social complexities of parenthood will have become too variable and indistinct to differentiate?"

The more important question is, "What will it mean to kids if this comes to pass?"

Suggested Questions for Discussion

1. Do you think you parents are different from each other? If you think so, how are they different?

2. Is the difference only because one is a male and the other a female?

3. If there are differences between them, are they important?

4. How do you feel about any differences between your parents?

5. Do any of the differences between them affect you?

6. Is there any difference between your parents in how they share their affection with you?

7. Do you get along better with your mother or your father? Why?

8. What do you think a mother should be like? Is your mother like that?

9. What do you think a father should be like? Is your father like that?

CHAPTER XIII

Parent Personalities

Just about anybody in our society can marry or live together unmarried and have children. There are no qualifying tests or personality profiles that must be met to determine whether couples are fit to live together, are a good match, or have the skills, knowledge, or temperament for raising children. It's pretty much any Tom, Dick, and Harry with a go at any Helen, Jane, and Mary. Thus the great jeopardy to children, whose welfare is left open to the considerable possibility of incompetence in those who become parents.

There have been all sorts of attempts by various cultures, both ancient and modern, to guarantee the success of marriage through religious sanctions and cultural traditions and to keep it inviolate in face of all the hazards that threaten its existence. Marriage so packaged by formula may be for the good of the state, but it is not necessarily advantageous to the creative growth of the married partners, particularly the wives and mothers, whose lives have been traditionally dominated by the husband.

Since most modern marriages are without such rigid religious and cultural guidelines, they must depend for their viability more on the rapport between husband and wife. In effect, that depends on the fair give and take of their personalities.

What, then, are the important elements of personalities that can assure the success of a couple as parents?

That is a question that kids of your age should ask of yourselves, as well as of your parents. Kids, after all, are the ones who, for the many years they live with their parents, are both the observers and recipients of their parents' behavior.

Whereas it may seem that only older kids can make a verbal assessment of the personalities of their parents, enough is now known about babies and small children to reveal that they, too, can be acutely conscious of the kind of parents they have.

For a long time pediatricians and child psychologists have observed that babies are expert in interpreting the emotional atmosphere in the home. By the baby's body movements, gestures, talk, or screams of joy or pain, a baby tells how parents are or are not getting along, even though it has no understanding of what the parents are saying. It is with these same emotional feelings of childhood that older kids respond when their parents reenact their old conflicts in the home. At that age, however, kids can be more verbally and physically dramatic in their responses and protests. In fact, they can start throwing things in anger.

It is not only a parent's head cold or sniffles that may be contagious to a child. The unloving and mean-tempered personality of a parent can be equally contagious. Colds and sniffles can be cured, but what a cruel parent can do to a child may never be remedied. The contrary can be just as true: Love, too, can be contagious, for loving parents make loving children.

It is not only overt cruel behavior that tells a child what kind of personality a parent has. Equally revealing is the parent who shares little if any emotion, whose personality is flat and unresponsive. The child, as a result, is cheated by receiving no feedback of feeling. The relationship between child and parent becomes a nonrelationship, a void, giving the baby no grip on what it is to have human emotions. With such a parent, this nonrelationship with a child can continue through adolescence.

Another type is the parents whose very life comes to depend on the child for happiness. In a paradoxical fashion, the child becomes the parent and the parent the child. Unable to fulfill the emotional needs of the parent, the child becomes terror-stricken by the impossible expectation thrust upon it. The child becomes a sad, solemn human being deprived of all feelings by an emotionally starved parent. Typically this is a parent who is unhappy in marriage or whose marriage has fallen apart and who has no one left to love but the child.

Still another parent is beset by ups and downs of joy and depression that can drive a child to distraction trying to go along on a roller coaster of erratic, unpredictable moods.

Some parents are obsessed with meticulousness and punctuality in running the life of the family. They are so consumed with administrative efficiency, the ritual of daily planning and scheduling of life controlled by the clock, that there is no time left for them to love and have fun with their children. This is a personality more fit for a factory manager than a parent.

In sharp contrast is the parent who is totally unstructured in the care of children and whose attitude is not to worry but just to make do: Everything will turn out all right in the end.

Kids are given no choice and must accept the parents they get—but only up to a point. If the personality of a parent seriously endangers a kid's welfare, it is the kid's right and only hope to seek the help of a competent psychologist, minister, or counselor as early as possible to prevent his or her life from being destroyed.

Parents need not be perfect, nor can they do as much as many of them would like. But neither should they make it impossible for their kids to be happy, productive human beings. That runs contrary to all the reasons for wanting to have kids in the first place.

Suggested Questions for Discussion

1. What do you think of the personalities of your parents?
2. Are your parents' personalities very different or much the same?

3. Which of the two personalities do you prefer? Why

4. How do you think you are affected by the kind of personalities they have?

5. Have their personalities changed much since you were a little child? How?

6. Have those changes been for the better or worse?

7. Are the personalities of your parents a good match?

8. Are their personalities the kind that make for good parents?

9. What are the good and bad aspects of your parents' personalities?

10. Is your personality more like your mother's or your father's?

11. Are you pleased or disappointed if your personality has any resemblance to either parent?

12. Do you feel that your personality is entirely different from that of either parent?

CHAPTER XIV

Can Parents Be Bad for You?

In foster and group homes, state and county youth centers, and child care shelters scattered across the country are millions of abused children whose parents have been bad for them.

It would have been better for these kids never to have been born, for many will go through life, if they live at all, as physically and emotionally destroyed human beings. Some are so severely injured by the brutal beatings of parents that they have suffered massive brain damage and do not know who they are, where they are, or if they are dead or alive.

Kids who should be in places of protective custody are not there today because many of them were never given the chance. They were murdered by their parents.

Tragic stories appear in the press almost daily of parents' cruelty to children. Many such tragedies are never reported because parents hide the deeds. It is now a common practice of hospitals to check carefully on children brought in for emergency treatment to determine whether their injuries are the result of beatings by the parents. Some badly injured kids could have been saved if brought to the hospital in time but never were seen because their parents feared criminal charges.

Why would a parent treat a child that way? Studies have shown that parents who are physically cruel to their children were themselves so abused when they were young. It is a learned behavior that carries on from one generation to the next, and these parents assume that it is an acceptable way to discipline kids.

Typically, cruel parents have a very poor self-image. They

see their child as they see themselves. Emotionally, they make no differentiation between parent and child. Thus, when deeply depressed and unhappy with themselves, they may not only kill themselves but their child as well, identifying the child with their own mental state. By ending their own misery, they believe they are also ending the misery of the child.

The title "parent" seems to some adults to confer complete ownership of their child. They believe they have the right to do whatever they wish with the child, much as they might with a pet dog. There are laws, of course, that protect a child from parental abuse, but the laws are almost impossible to enforce without convincing proof.

Because society affirms the right of parents to punish a child physically as part of the responsibility to discipline the child, it becomes a difficult and touchy issue for society to decide when physical punishment becomes physical abuse. Some parents charged with child abuse, for instance, have countered that they were only disciplining the child, when, in fact, they had lost control in a fit of anger and had given the child a brutal thrashing. Some parents justify severe beating of children because their religious beliefs hold that the devil is inside a naughty child and must be driven out by physical force.

How serious must a child's physical injuries be to abrogate the right of a parent to punishment or to charge a parent with child abuse? And who is to know how serious the injuries are unless the child is taken to a doctor or hospital for treatment? And what parent who brutalized his or her child would seek medical help if doing so could result in a jail sentence?

As parents can be symbiotic (in close union) with their kids in their feelings, so also can kids be symbiotic with their parents. Indeed, kids retain throughout life this intimate interaction and interweaving of their emotions with those of their parents. Should the parent be very seriously disturbed and abusive, a kid can be traumatized for life and be unable to function adequately as a human being. Emotionally sick and abusive parents can and do make kids emotionally sick. What such a parent needs is professional care in a hospital, not to be left in the home for a kid to have to cope with.

If physical abuse of a kid by a parent is hard to prove, psychological abuse is almost impossible to prove against a parent. Yet the consequences of the one can be as damaging to a kid as the other.

A subtle form of psychological abuse is for a parent, under the guise of moral guidance, never to give a kid any approval or credit, only constant verbal abuse and criticism. This is a parent who browbeats a kid into submission to parental authority.

The vulnerability of kids to the great damage parents can do to them requires that parents be very special people—the best possible of human beings. Their personal qualities and behavior must be of a higher order than those that might do in the outside world, in the office or on the street. If they are not, then for their own good as well as for the welfare of their children, parents should seek professional help.

What should kids do whose parents physically or psychologically abuse them? It is a decision kids have to make for themselves, perhaps with the help of a family or school counselor, a community counseling service, or the minister of their church.

Physical or psychological abuse by parents is not a burden that any kid should have to carry through life. Nor should any parent who abuses kids be allowed to escape full punishment for such behavior.

Suggested Questions for Discussion

1. Do you think your parents are bad for you; that is, are they mean and cruel to you—even beat you? If you think so, what are your reasons?

2. If your parents are mean and cruel to you, why do you think they are? Have you ever discussed it with them?

3. Have your parents always been this way to you? If not, why have they changed? Have you ever asked them, or is that too hard for you to do?

4. If your parents do not physically abuse you, do they psychologically abuse you; that is, call you nasty names, never say anything good about you, treat you unkindly most of the time?

5. If your parents do abuse you, physically or psychologically or both, how do you protect yourself? Have you turned to anyone for help? If not, why not?

6. If you have kind and loving parents, are there any kids you know who are abused by their parents? Have you ever tried to help them by being their friend and suggesting where they can get professional help?

CHAPTER XV

Do Parents Make Good Friends?

Parents do make good friends with their kids, some to the day they die. But there are also many parents who never have good relations with their kids to the day they die.

It would seem the most natural thing in the world for parents and kids to get along with each other and be good friends, for what greater closeness could there be than that which binds them together from the moment kids are born? These strong ties are evident wherever there is birth, from the highest to the lowest forms of mammals.

What is also evident is that there is a loosening of these ties as kids grow older and no longer want to rely on their parents for everything they think and do. It is at this stage that the friendship between parents and kids is seriously threatened. Rather than accept this change in their kids as the normal transition to becoming adults, many parents are dismayed at the loss of a relationship they had when their kids were little.

Does this growing separation of kids from parents necessarily mean that they can no longer be good friends? It is not only that grown kids no longer want to be dependent on them that distresses parents. Of greater concern are the changes in the beliefs and attitudes that parents have taught their kids to cherish. That is the real heartache that can lead to estrangement from their kids.

Whether parents will or will not continue to be good friends with their kids is up to the parents. It is a question of how strongly they feel about the beliefs that their kids have rejected and those that they have adopted instead. It is difficult and sometimes impossible for parents to continue a warm friendship with kids who hold opinions contrary to their own.

Some inflexible parents may not realize it, but to expect older kids to continue to think and believe as they do, and not to develop their own outlook on life, is to expect them to remain at an infantile stage. It may be comforting for such parents to have grown kids who do not question their beliefs but adhere to parental ways. But what does that do to the kids? What credit can they rightly expect from parents for holding ideas or viewpoints that their parents claim as their own?

With such conformity there is little opportunity for kids to establish their own individuality. Ironically, it is this very duplication of their parents' way of life that can earn them lack of respect by parents. These kids can serve as both unflattering and flattering mirrors in which parents see themselves glaringly reflected with all their shortcomings and frailties, along with what they like to believe are their strengths.

Whether parents can be good friends with their kids rests solely with the parents. If they have not been warm, kind, fun-loving, and understanding with their kids from the start, they are not likely to make friends of their kids when they are older. If they are also dogmatic and inflexible human beings, it may be impossible for them to be friends of their kids. Neither will they be successful if they resent, rather than honor and respect, the right of their kids to determine their own way of life. If parents want respect, they must first show respect to their kids, especially when the kids have ideas and beliefs contrary to their own.

Why do some parents not make friends with their kids? That is a question you should ask of your parents if you feel that they are no longer your friends. It is important to get the answers so that you do not go through life feeling that possibly it was your fault, not theirs, that this happened. Perhaps, too, by having such a discussion with your parents you might salvage your friendship and make your home a happy place again.

Suggested Questions for Discussion

1. Are you and your parents good friends? If not, why not?
2. Have you and your parents always been good friends?
3. Has your friendship with your parents changed since you have grown older?
4. If there has been a change, what is the change? What caused it?
5. If you are no longer good friends, has anything been done to restore your friendship?
6. Have those attempts failed or succeeded?
7. If there is no friendship between you and your parents, how has that affected your lives, if at all?
8. Does it make any difference to you and your parents whether you are good friends or not?

CHAPTER XVI

Working Mothers

One of the principal responsibilities of parents has always been to earn enough money to support the family. In fact, most of their time is spent in doing just that. To carry out this obligation becomes especially worrying when bad economic times make it difficult, and sometimes impossible, for them to do so.

Our country has experienced enough depressions and recessions to know what it is for parents to be out of a job and what suffering and hardship that means for the family. No parent takes comfort or pride in having to apply for food stamps or stand in lines to get a handout to feed the family.

In the middle-class home it has been traditional for the father to be the breadwinner of the family. The job of the mother was to stay at home, care for the house, cook the meals, and raise the kids. Among the poor, this was less true. Since the father of the family was a so-called common laborer who could not earn enough money to support the family, the mother had to work. At that time the only work available to her was as a washerwoman, a seamstress, or a maid. As much as possible she tried to get work that would not take her out of the home, such as doing laundry, sewing, and dressmaking, so she could still be on hand to take care of the home and especially her children.

Today, the role of both women and mothers in all economic groups has changed radically and is continuing to change at a rapid pace. More mothers than ever before now work outside the home and in jobs and professions that have always been the exclusive domain of men: doctors, dentists, lawyers, administrators. Even in jobs that are considered to require physical strength and stamina—construction, carpentry, auto repair, heavy industry—mothers are appearing in growing numbers. Increasingly, they are also seen as political leaders and in government. This change of status is particularly startling in light of the fact that it was only a little over sixty years ago that women were first allowed to vote.

What has brought about this change in the role of mothers in our society? Mothers no longer want to fill the sole role of homemaker. They feel that they have too long been in bondage to men by being relegated to household chores and raising kids. They now demand that their traditional role henceforth be shared equally with their husbands. A new world opened to them. They discovered that they have skills and abilities equal to men and that their competence can bring them the same satisfaction that men have claimed as their sole right and privilege.

This "new" mother can be seen in growing numbers in colleges and universities, in business and professional schools, in the health, physical, and biological sciences, in computer technology, and in technical schools that until a few years ago were largely reserved for men. In politics, where women represent the largest bloc of voters, they have gained a recognition and power that would have been unthinkable only a few years ago. Yet, with all the gains they have made, they still have a long way to go to undo the countless laws and restrictions to their freedom that have accumulated over generations and that still exist in our predominantly male-dominated society.

To retain their own individuality and avoid being compromised by the marriage contract, many working mothers retain their maiden names and keep their bank account separate from that of their husband. Some even maintain a separate household although they are married and have children.

While this new-found freedom of mothers has opened up

countless doors to the outside world for them, what about their children? How has it affected them? Unfortunately, their situation has received the least attention.

That should come as no surprise. It is, after all, the adults who have the power to initiate and determine changes in society, often without ever considering whether they are good or bad for kids.

Kids will probably have to adjust to the changes as parents grope their way to what they see as a more equitable arrangement between them and decide what are their responsibilities to their kids.

Suggested Questions for Discussion

1. If your mother works outside the home, does she have to work to help support the family? Explain.

2. If your mother works outside the home, does she receive the same pay and privileges that men receive for the same or comparable work? If not, why not?

3. Is it hard for your mother to hold a job and also take care of the family and the home?

4. Do others in the family help her out with family chores? How?

5. Is your family like some families where the mother is the breadwinner and the father the homemaker? If so, what do you think about this reversal in the traditional roles of parents?

6. If your mother works only to have a career of her own, do you think she should? Why or why not?

7. Does the time your mother gives to her career bring satisfaction or only hardship to the family?

8. Is it important for a mother to have a career even if it means some inconveniences or hardship to the family?

9. Were you consulted about your mother's career plans before she took a job? If not, do you think you should have been consulted? If you were, were your opinions seriously considered by your mother?

10. Is it fair that only the mother, not the father, should be faced with the choice of having or not having a career if the career brings hardship to the family? What is your viewpoint?

11. If both of your parents have careers, do those careers affect their relationship?

12. If their separate careers have caused problems between your parents, how have they been resolved, if at all?

CHAPTER XVII

Who Holds the Purse Strings?

Historically, the person who earned the money in the family was the one who controlled the family. That was especially true when the father was the main wage earner, and in many families it is still so. Even though the mother worked as hard and put in many more hours as a homemaker than her husband did at his work outside the home, she had little if anything to say about how the family's money was to be spent. What money wives did receive from their husbands was doled out grudgingly, even for the most basic needs of the family, along with a demand for a strict accounting of every penny spent. Since money in society is power, influence, and control, it was not likely to be much different in the family.

Some wives under this patriarchal system did not always give in easily to their husband's control of the purse strings. Fights over money were common. To avoid these domestic battles, from which the husband usually came out the victor, clever wives devised all kinds of ways to get around their spouse, for example, by hiding household money that they claimed to have spent so that they could buy things their husband would not allow them to have.

This subjugation of the wife to the husband was self-perpetuating so long as the husband was the major source of income for the family. Today, much of that power has come to an end with the advent of more than half the wives into the labor market. Now they, too, can claim that their pay is theirs to do with as they wish. The power structure of the family is being shared by wives and husbands, mothers and fathers. Both hold the purse strings.

Some husbands still find it difficult to accept financial equality with their wives in running the family. They would like to return to total control, even though they recognize that the family could not stay financially afloat without the earnings of their wife. Indeed, they resent the fact that they have to depend on that income to pay the bills.

With both parents working and bringing money into the family, if there is a difference of opinion over how money is to be spent or saved, the husband can no longer coerce the wife by threatening to cut off all funds to the family. The husband must now be willing to compromise.

To protect their bargaining position with obdurate husbands, some wives have their savings and checking accounts in their name only, not held jointly with the husband, who in a fit of anger might appropriate them. In this way, wives also protect their funds should they be divorced and need to support themselves and any children who live with them.

As kids know, parents still argue over money despite the fact that both now hold the family purse strings. Statistically, money causes more family arguments than any other issue. Kids themselves may be involved in these disputes when it comes to deciding how much money they will receive as an allowance.

Parental arguments at least over money are fairer now that both earn money and must decide together how it is to be spent. Whether this is done successfully and without acrimony depends on the respect and love the parents have for each other. If there is love between them, there is warm sharing and giving and no need to make the home an arena for two wage earners fighting for power.

The tough, competitive world in which parents work is not a world to come home from feeling warm and loving, any more than one could feel warm and loving returning from a battlefield after a hard-fought war. The family requires cooperation, not competition, for the strength and love it needs.

The business world demands ruthless competition and aggression to achieve that power called money. The world outside and the world inside the home are two different and often opposing worlds. It is the responsibility of parents not confuse the two. It is one thing for them to share in holding the purse strings in the home; it is quite something else to strangle each other with them.

Suggested Questions for Discussion

1. Who do you think holds the purse strings in your family? Why do you think so?

2. If it is one parent, why do you think that is so?

3. Do both parents hold the purse strings and share equally in disposition of family funds?

4. Do your parents argue over money? If so, what specifically do they argue about?

5. How do they resolve any differences they may have over money? Are the solutions or compromises good ones, or do they result in further resentment?

6. Do you think your parents handle the family finances wisely? If not, why not?

7. Does it make any difference which parent earns the most in determining how the family money is used?

8. Do you think your parents are careful or irresponsible with the family money?

9. Are you involved in any of the decisions on how the family money is to be saved or spent?

10. If you receive an allowance, who decides the amount you receive? Are you allowed to participate in the decision? If not, why not?

11. Do you think the amount of your allowance is fair? Give your reasons.

12. Do you think your parents budget their money wisely? Do they budget their money at all?

13. Have you learned by the example of your parents how to handle your own money to best advantage?

CHAPTER XVIII

Parents as Citizens

As parents must earn money to support the family, so should they participate in government to see that it serves the best interests of the family. What happens in local, state, and federal government has a big impact on the welfare and security of the family. Parents alone do not determine the fate of the family.

It hardly needs saying that government policies concerning education, taxation, employment, job security, fiscal practices, trade, health and welfare, peace, and war play critical roles in the life of the family. Nor should it have to be said that the failure of parents to take part in deciding these issues can negate all the good they have done for the family.

Participation in government, however, requires hard work. It demands that parents be informed and knowledgeable about all issues, monitor the legislative process, and be active in opposing or supporting legislation through political action and the ballot box on election day. All that takes time and effort and money, but it is how the democratic process works, and it is the responsibility of a good citizen. It is not enough to be a conscientious parent. A parent must also be a conscientious citizen.

Neither is it enough for kids to learn the ABC's of government in school books. They must also have parents who take an active part in the democratic process to show them that the system we live under and cherish works as the textbooks say it does. Without such parents, how can kids make any connection between what they learn in the classroom and what takes place in the real world of politics. How can they appreciate the importance of being involved in the democratic process if their own parents are nonparticipants?

It is startling to realize that of all eligible voters, of whom parents make up the majority, less than half actually vote on election day. That means that most officeholders, including the President of the United States, are elected by default, by the failure of over half the eligible voters to vote. It means that if most of the eligible voters in the last election had voted, we might have different people in office than we now have, including the President. We would also possibly have very different policies and programs directing the course of the country.

Even if all the parents in the country voted, how many of them would be sufficiently well informed to vote intelligently on candidates and referenda on the ballot? At the last moment on election day, for instance, how many parents search the morning newspaper to find out how they should vote? As for the list of judges to be elected, how many parents know enough about their legal training and background and the record of their court decisions to be in any position to make choices that would help to create a more just and honest judicial system?

An examination of the returns of any election shows that most voters do not even vote for judges because they have taken no time to learn anything about them. Voters mostly choose candidates for political office with whom they have some familiarity. Often the choices are made along party lines even though there may be better candidates in the opposing party.

Being an informed voter, however, is the minimum requirement to qualify parents as good citizens. They must undertake many activities if they are to influence legislation that will benefit the family and the country. These include writing letters, sending telegrams, and sponsoring petitions to urge their Senators and Representatives to support specific legislation.

Contributions of money are also needed to help defray the heavy expenses of candidates who run for office.

Why, one has to ask, is there so little participation by parents in the political process? Why do so many parents not bother to vote?

Unfortunately, many parents have grown cynical about what difference their efforts can make. They feel that the small guy has no chance with a Congress controlled by the big guys with the big money. Then, all the scandals about corruption in government that appear almost daily in the press shake their confidence in the integrity of our political system. As a result, many parents become discouraged and give up.

With such feelings of alienation, how can parents serve as examples of good citizenship to their kids? Having given up hope in democracy, they dismiss political action as the naive notion of those who are gullible enough to believe that they can effect changes for the better in government.

But isn't that what all the school books tell the kids they *can* do?

Suggested Questions for Discussion

1. Do you think your parents are good citizens? Why or why not?

2. Do you think your parents do their share in participating in the political process?

3. Are your parents conscientious and informed voters?

4. Are your parents helping you to become a thoughtful and active citizen in government?

5. Do your parents freely discuss political and social issues with you?

6. If your parents are inactive or even negative about their responsibilities as citizens, why do you think they are? Do you or do you not agree with their attitude? Why?

CHAPTER XIX

Parents Don't Stay the Same

As you have changed since you were a small child, so have your parents changed as they have grown older. You may not have paid much attention to this fact; like most kids your age, you are likely to be more interested in yourself as a rapidly growing person than in anyone else. It is easy for kids to take parents for granted, along with the furniture, three meals a day, and a bed at night.

Parents can be as interested in what is happening to their bodies as boys are intrigued by the early signs of adulthood with the appearance of a beard and girls with the growth of their breasts. However, it is with more apprehension than anticipation that parents observe the tell-tale changes in their physical appearance with approaching age. For the fathers it can be a receding hairline or a bald spot as they study themselves in the bathroom mirror, or a sagging belly over the belt. For the mothers there are those first little wrinkles at the eyes and neck, a slight graying at the temples, and perhaps an embarrassing broadening of the hips and thighs.

With the high premium placed by society on youth and a youthful appearance, and the fears that adults have of aging, it is no surprise that many parents lavish inordinate sums of money and time on beauty parlors, health spas, and diet clinics. Behind what can become a frantic dedication to physical fitness lies a secret hope that they can stay the inexorable hand of time, perhaps even postpone indefinitely their own demise. Health can become a fetish when the fear of death becomes an obsession.

Some parents become so intense about their own interests,

whether for health, spiritual, or philosophical reasons or to gain personal acclaim and recognition, that they neglect the well-being of their kids. With the breakup of families so prevalent today has come an equal neglect of kids by self-centered, self-indulgent parents. They exist detached from commitment to anyone but themselves, seeking aimlessly for their so-called identity in phony cults, false messiahs, and psychic dead-ends that have proliferated across the country. It is as though these parents had never known or been taught the simple ABC's of finding their own true value in being good parents to their kids. It is a sad day when parents no longer recognize this. It will be a sadder time for kids, who will have to pay for this neglect throughout their lives.

In the meantime, what happens to these kids? If the parents float, the kids float, equally mindless and confused. Kids do no more than reflect the world of their parents unless they have the good sense and strength to be able to reject that crazy world.

Despite the considerable family disorientation extant today, there are still level-headed parents who love each other and their kids and who are ready, in the face of great odds, to do everything in their power to help their family. To them, being a parent is a vocation, not an avocation. Their first and most important commitment is to the home, not their job or career or hobby or social life. Parenting, to them, is not something to be pursued or not pursued according to personal whim. It is a serious ethical obligation they owe their children, whom they alone are responsible for bringing into the world.

These are parents who can suffer through recessions, depressions, natural disasters, serious illness, loss of job, death in the family, poverty, and accidents and still keep the family together with love and devotion and even joy.

The question often arises, "Are there certain definite stages or phases of change that parents go through? If so, when and why do they happen and what do they mean to the family?"

The changes parents go through, from the birth of a child until it is old enough to be on its own, have to do with a variety of life experiences that are common to most human beings, parent or nonparent. Like anyone else, parents can be sick or well, poor or well off, suffer failures, enjoy successes, and experience all of the many other happy or sad fortunes in life. What makes it especially hard for parents is the impact that these common experiences, especially the negative ones, can have on the family and on the kids.

Is divorce a typical phase and an inevitable part of being a parent? Currently it seems so because of the large number of divorces taking place today. It is impossible to predict whether the present trend will continue or subside in the years ahead. It may be that the number of divorces, rather than the fact of divorce, will diminish.

Two comparatively new factors have arisen during the present generation that could be called new phases or changes in parenthood: (1) more mothers than ever before are working outside the home; and (2) the number of single parents living alone or with their children is growing rapidly.

These changes have been brought about by the growing demand of mothers for the same right as husbands to have a career outside the home and to receive equal pay and treatment in the world of work. Wives also want husbands to share in the care and training of children and in the household chores that have always been the primary lot of mothers.

What will these changes mean to kids in the family? It is too early to tell. What is sure is that if the parents love each other and share that love with the kids, the changes in the roles of parents will be much less traumatic. They can even be taken in stride by everyone in the family. If there is neglect of the kids because of parental conflict over their role changes, only injury to all can result.

If kids are to have any chance in life, parents may change their roles but not their love for each other and the family.

Suggested Questions for Discussion

1. Do you think your parents have changed very much since you were little? How did they change, if at all?

2. Has each parent changed in a different way?

3. Do you like how your parents have changed?

4. Do you think your parents think more of themselves than they do of you?

5. Are your parents happy with how you have changed?

6. Do you think your family has changed for the better or worse since you were little?

CHAPTER XX

When Tragedy Strikes

Never does a family show how vulnerable it is more than when tragedy strikes. It is the vulnerability of an entity made strong by the interdependence of each member of the family, but which paradoxically is made dangerously weak by the sheer weight of the interdependence that burdens every member.

The fragility of this family structure can be seen by the distress that arises in some homes over the minutiae of daily living: burnt toast at breakfast, a bad day at the office, a gravy stain on the tablecloth, no toilet paper in the john, mud on the carpet, a sneeze that means a cold, no hot water, a missing sock, no butter, spilt milk, a check that bounced.

If such niggling problems can shake the family structure, what happens when its very foundation, the bond of love between the parents, begins to crumble? The results can be catastrophic for all. The grieving becomes its own illness, infecting every member of the family, some for life.

The causes of family tragedies are as numerous as the failings of man. Being a parent does not make one any less prone to all the frailties man is heir to: alcoholism, mental illness, drug addiction, suicide, deceit, adultery, incest, physical and mental abuse, even murder. Actually, more violence and killing goes on in the home than anywhere else, except for the battlefield.

Some cruel blows are dealt the family for which you cannot in all fairness hold your parents responsible, such as serious illnesses, accidents, crippling injuries and disabilities, the ravages of war, and poverty. Sometimes kids can cope better

with those than with the tragic happenings for which they feel
parents can rightly be held responsible.

It is not always easy to determine which kinds of family
tragedies do the most harm to kids. Is it harder to lose a
mother or father in a fatal accident than as a result of divorce?
Because of cancer, than as a convicted criminal? Because of
mental illness, than because of desertion?

Also important are considerations of personal differences,
age, time, place, and circumstances that can play a crucial role
in how family tragedies affect you. If you have experienced
any deep emotional blows in your family, only you can know
what they have meant to you.

Perhaps the most hurtful circumstance for kids is to live
day in and day out with parents who are dishonest with themselves and with their kids. To cover up their faults and frailties, such parents resort to lies and subterfuge to deceive the
kids. The tragic results of such dissimulation can only be
bitterness and cynicism as kids painfully uncover the truth
and have to live with a sick charade.

The youth rebellion of the 60's and 70's was the result of a
national rejection of what young people saw as the dishonest
and pretentious values of their elders. What followed was a
mass tragedy for both parents and kids that has left the American family is disarray to this day.

Kids want to know the truth about parents so that they can
make some sense out of a world they have not been allowed to
understand.

It is no longer, "Timmy, you must always tell the truth." It
is now, "Dad, Mom, you also must tell the truth."

If parents are to retain the respect of their kids, they must
be open with them. If parents want a divorce, the kids want to
know why. If parents have arguments and fights, the kids
want to know why. If a parent becomes mentally ill, a felon,
an alcoholic, or a drug addict, is depressed or unhappy, is
having an affair, the kids want to know why as honestly as

parents can tell them. And if parents do not know the answer themselves or are unable to bring themselves to tell their kids, someone else should do it, preferably a family counselor.

Suggested Questions for Discussion

1. Have any great sorrows seriously hurt your family? What were they?
2. Were your parents responsible for any of them? Why?
3. Could they have been avoided? How?
4. How did your parents cope with them? Did they help you to do so? How?
5. Which of these tragedies do you think hurt you the most? Why?
6. Do you see your parents differently as a result of any family tragedies? Why?
7. Are your parents open and truthful with you about their own weaknesses or failures, or do they try to cover them up?

CHAPTER XXI

When Parents Stop Loving Each Other

How does it happen that parents can stop loving each other? When they first fell in love they certainly had no thought that a day might come when they would no longer love each other. Love then was expected to last for life.

All lovers want their love to last forever. That is why the great love stories of literature have such a strong appeal to us. Through them we relive and renew our hope for a lasting love.

Those stories are also tragic tales of lovers torn from each other by death, by war, and by forces and events beyond their control. In these tragedies there is always the accusing finger pointing, if not at fate, certainly at a cruel and ruthless society that destroys the dreams and hopes of lovers.

Older married couples cynically taunt newlyweds with the saying, "The honeymoon is over,"meaning that from now on there will be no time to enjoy the luxury of being in love. Henceforth their life will be spent in the drudgery of trying to earn a living and run a household. If they also take on the burden of becoming parents and raising a family, there will be very little time indeed for their romantic love.

During the best of economic times, parental responsibilities are difficult enough for any couple in love. In hard economic times, however, the burden can be devastating. Daily living becomes a grim battle to keep the family fed and clothed. Poverty can be a killer of families and a killer of what little love parents may have left for each other.

But what happens to parents' love even when times are good? What are the rational explanations for so many parents breaking up as they are doing today?

It would be enlightening if one could document the step-by-step, incident-by-incident deterioration of the love between parents that led to the dissolution of their marriage. If you asked divorced parents how it was that they stopped loving each other, they probably would be unable to give you an answer. It would be as hard for them to pinpoint when and how it happened as it might be for a Wall Street broker to tell you just when and how an economic recession began and when it ended.

Almost unknowingly, their love disintegrated, bit by bit, over the hours, day, months, and years so that they were unaware of what was happening or when it began to die. Sometimes all that remains is for them to catch up to the hard reality that it died long ago.

Parents who no longer love each other often say that their love ended quite suddenly and without warning when they learned that the other parent had a lover all along. The only explanation of this ignorance of what was going on is their reluctance to admit that they no longer loved each other. The shock and surprise are a pretext of the injured parent who failed to face up to that fact much earlier and do something about it.

In earlier chapters attention was given to how the love of young married couples can be threatened by serious differences over family beliefs and backgrounds and differences in their individual personalities. It was pointed out that if these potentially divisive issues are not resolved they can endanger and even end the relationship. The same can be said if parents allow their jobs and social activities to come between them. When the outside world becomes more important than the world inside the home, their marriage is in serious trouble.

Parents can easily be seduced into sacrificing their love for each other and for the family in order to become big in business, an outstanding professional person, a great athlete, actor, or musician, or a social leader in the community. The rationalizations these parents make to justify the neglect of each other and the family are designed to assuage their guilt. Dad says he needs to spend more late hours at the club with his business associates to win friends and gain a promotion so that he can make more money for the family. Mom joins the community actors' guild to raise money for worthy causes. She decides to take acting classes, try out for more parts, take speech classes, even if it means that Dad and the kids will hardly see her anymore. Then there are all those worthwhile social causes to save the world for parents to throw themselves into with an energy and dedication that can even astonish their children, if not dismay them, and make them feel that it is they, not the world, that need saving.

Because of their heavy commitments to pursuits outside the home to satisfy their strong ego needs, parents are often unaware of how much they are neglecting each other. The deterioration in their relationship is marked by their sensitivity to any criticism of their outside activities and by bitter words over the need for them to spend more time with each other.

Does this mean that parents can never follow interests outside the home without destroying their love for each other and the family?

Some parents are able to do both, to love each other and also carry on interests outside the home. Not everyone, however, is able to play this dual role successfully. If undertaken, such a demanding schedule must be carefully monitored to see that parents do not alienate themselves from each other and their children.

This high-wire balancing act can pose a real challenge and danger. For a parent not to lose his or her balance requires enormous skill and agility that many parents may not possess. Sometimes it shows down-to-earth good sense for a parent to get off the high wire before he or she falls off and the whole family has to share in the almost impossible task of trying to put Mom, Dad, and the kids back together again.

Suggested Questions for Discussion

1. Are your parents still in love with each other? How do you know?

2. Does one parent show more love than the other?

3. Has their love for each other changed since you were little? If so, how has it changed?

4. Are you afraid that they might stop loving each other?

5. If your parents do not love each other as much as they once did, why do you think this happened? What do you think should be done?

6. If they are not getting along together, do you think you should discuss that with them?

CHAPTER XXII

Infidelity

With the current laissez-faire attitude toward marriage or living together unmarried that has resulted in a high divorce and separation rate, it should come as no surprise that there also exists a high rate of infidelity among parents. While the rate among married men has always been somewhat higher than among women, that gap is closing rapidly. About 44 percent of married women have had extramarital affairs.

Out of fear of being trapped in the locked-in marriage of previous generations, when infidelity was hidden behind a facade of false respectability, many parents bend over backwards to see that neither husband nor wife is constrained by required fidelity. Both can now be free and open in a relationship where there are no longer any prohibitions against having love partners outside of marriage.

What has taken place is the erosion of the dominant role of the husband as the one who literally and legally possessed the wife and demanded her total faithfulness while he could carry on his own love affairs with impunity.

With the new freedom, many parents no longer consider infidelity a problem. How can there be a problem when fidelity is no longer required? In fact, the free-wheeling behavior now evident among some parents openly declares the freedom, the right, and even the need for parents to seek love outside of marriage. It is their conviction that only by avoiding the dishonesty and deceit so prevalent in marriages of the past can parents strengthen their own relationship.

Given this viewpoint, many questions arise: Can parents carry on extramarital love affairs, whether openly or secretly, and still love each other? Is there a right or wrong way of love? Why is there a need for other lovers when parents love each other? Has it come to the point where the only way parents can prove their love for each other is by having affairs with others? Does the freedom or need to do so become more important than their love for each other? Is the fear of giving yourself to one person so great that to do so becomes a heresy? Has fidelity now become infidelity?

Jealousy has been an emotion common to lovers throughout human history. It is not likely to disappear from the lives of men and women, husbands and wives, mothers and fathers, despite its present characterization as old-fashioned. It is an emotion that has served men and women well, protecting and giving stability to lovers, safeguarding mating and the birth and care of children. When the security of any of those stages in the development of the family is threatened, jealousy can become not only protective but violently protective, and even deadly, in its mission.

There are, however, many parents who still believe in being faithful to each other. If they become unfaithful, it is likely to happen during a falling-out or before a divorce. Another possibility of infidelity for such parents is when one of them has to be away from home for a time and misses love-making so much that he or she has an affair with some chance acquaintance.

Is that pardonable? Some parents think so. They forgive, but often with a deep and unspoken hurt that will always remain with them. But what of the parent who has to be away from home on business frequently and for long periods of time? Should such a parent who makes extramarital affairs a practice also be pardoned? Would it be best for this parent to keep such unfaithfulness a secret to prevent hurt? But does any of this help the relationship? Would it not be best to avoid such a job, well-paying as it might be, to avoid destroying the family?

Fidelity is not just a matter of honesty between parents. It is a matter of fairness to each other and the kids.

Suggested Questions for Discussion

1. Has either of your parents been unfaithful? If so, do you know why?

2. If either or both parents are unfaithful, is it common knowledge in the family or do the parents try to keep it a secret?

3. If only one of your parents is unfaithful, what does the other feel or do about it?

4. Do your parents believe that to have outside love affairs is not wrong and needs no explanation or justification?

5. Does it make any difference to you if your parents are unfaithful?

6. Do you think it hurts kids when parents are unfaithful?

CHAPTER XXIII

Divorce

Only a few years ago divorce was a scandal that led to the social ostracism of the family in the community. Today it is seen as something that can happen to anyone, like getting a cold or a parking ticket.

The high incidence of divorce has made it no longer an occurrence of social or moral significance, but a nonevent of no ethical consequence. Churches that once railed against it with great moral indignation now accept it as a reality of life. Few sermons against divorce are heard from the Sunday pulpit. Divorce has become a way of life tht society as a whole has come to accept.

Society has also removed most of the legal roadblocks that once made divorce so difficult and expensive. A divorce can now be legally concluded with the convenience and speed of a fast-food meal. Nor need it require complicated hassles over money and property if the couple agrees not to contest the divorce. This is called a no-fault divorce. Couples today prefer such a procedure to the long emotion-draining experience that divorce once represented.

But why so much divorce? Why the change from a time when divorce was rare and viewed as a social stigma to a time when it is insignificant in the eyes of society?

Much of the change has resulted from the growing rebellion of women during the last and present generations against a male-dominated society that controlled their lives both in and outside the home. Wives and mothers felt hostage to their husbands, who, with the support of the church and the courts, made it almost impossible for them to get a divorce despite the most flagrant and cruel behavior they suffered at the hands of their husbands.

The children of those marriages were also disenchanted by what they saw as the false morality and hypocrisy of the family with its emphasis on financial success and absence of any qualities of fairness, love, and humanity. It was they, today's adults, who in the 60's and 70's set out to tear down the pretentious facade of the family and to institute instead the social, legal, and moral changes we now see taking place in society. These were the kids who were called "flower children" because of their mission of kindness, honesty, and peace, as symbolized by the flowers they carried during their public demonstrations.

Often with social change, there is a difficult transition from what people do not want to what they do want. The "do not want" is always clearer than the "want." The latter is uncharted territory into which people who seek change are suddenly propelled by unanticipated forces in getting rid of what they do not want.

No longer would there be a problem, thought these architects of a new society, in getting out of a marriage you did not want. If you feared that what had happened to your parents might happen to you, you avoided getting married. Lovers could live together as well, and perhaps even better, without a marriage license.

It all seemed so easy and simple that many of the rebels assumed there would be no further problems between men and women living together and having children.

But all did not turn out as hoped. Human love cannot be treated with simplistic formulas. Deep hurt can result to lovers, whether married or unmarried, if each thinks only of himself or herself and not of the needs of the other or their children. That was exactly what happened. Each did his or her own thing first. As a result, families fell apart.

The epidemic of divorce also took its toll among older couples, who began to question the value of their many years of life together. The fact that people were living longer than ever before increased the chances that a prolonged relationship could become sterile.

Throughout this difficult and confusing transition in the relationship between men and women, husbands and wives, little concern was given to how it affected the lives of the kids. As a consequence, the period, which still continues today, has become one of the worst ever known for its indifference, neglect, and even abuse of kids. Kids are dragged from one household to another by all kinds of assumed fathers and mothers who know nothing about being parents or even about themselves. How can kids have any security when their parents have none?

So the long search goes on and, from all evidence, may go on for a long time, with muddled parents hauling their kids from cult to cult, commune to commune, from one religion to another, from messiah to messiah, in search of an answer that might help them learn again what it is to believe and love each other.

Once it seemed a simple answer that most parents thought they knew. Now it appears it no longer is.

Suggested Questions for Discussion

1. If your parents are not separated or divorced, do you worry that they might be someday?

2. Are there any signs that give you reason to be worried that your parents might leave each other?

3. If your parents are planning on leaving each other, have they given you an explanation of why they are going to do so?

4. Are you free to discuss all aspects of the proposed divorce or separation with your parents? Are your parents responsive to what you ask or say?

5. Do your parents want the divorce or separation equally, or is it primarily the desire of just one parent?

6. Do you think your parents did everything in their power, for instance, saw a marriage counselor or family psychologist, to prevent the divorce or separation from taking place? Did they do so early enough to be able to resolve their problems before it was too late?

7. Do you agree or disagree with your parents' reasons for getting a divorce?

8. How does the decision of your parents to leave each other affect you? Are your parents fully aware of your feelings? How are they helping you, if at all, through this period?

9. What are your parents' plans for you following the divorce? Were you included in the discussions and decisions of what arrangements would be best for you? Are you satisfied with the plans made for you?

CHAPTER XXIV

New Moms and Dads

The long dependence that kids have on adults continues whether they have real parents or not. If one parent dies, the other usually takes over the responsibility. If both die, relatives or friends step in or the state takes over through foster care or residence in a group home.

Adoption is also a possibility. It is more likely for very young children or infants, who are preferred by couples who are unable to have their own children. An adopted baby is small and young enough so that the adopting parents can easily feel it is their own.

Most substitute parents, the new moms and dads, are stepparents, single or divorced men and women, who may or may not have their own children from a previous union and now live together as a new family.

The question always comes up, "Are stepparents better than real parents?"

If you have lived through such a situation, you probably pondered that question sometime before or soon after you began living with stepparents. And, as you began to find out, it is the quality of the adult with whom you live that counts, not the title of the relationship. It is unfortunate but true that being a real parent is not always a guarantee that a person is a good, loving human being. Because of the deep emotional ties with a real parent, however, there is no greater hurt for a child than to have a real parent who is a bad human being. It is a hurt that is never easy for a kid to get over, even after he or she is grown up.

Because of the emotional problems that often result from

such a relationship with a bad parent, such kids are not likely to be adopted, and if they are, they are not easily assimilated into a new family with other children.

Kids who have gone through any of this know the story better than anyone, for many of them have written a good part of it in their own unhappy daily lives wherever they are. Perhaps you may be one of them.

But what do the real parents say of their lost kids from broken homes and divorce? Most of them are loath to admit how poorly they have handled the family relationship for which their children have paid so dearly. The sorrow can be even further compounded, as it too often is, when the new moms and dads don't work out either. Then there are still other new moms and dads to whom kids must adjust.

The fact is that there is no good substitute for your own parents who gave you birth and who love and nurture you as they love and nurture each other as husband and wife. All else is first aid or major surgery that may or may not help a kid from a broken home.

Suggested Questions for Discussion

1. Why is it that kids today have so many new moms and dads? Is this good or bad for kids?

2. What reasons, if any, do parents use to justify making family changes? Should or could such changes be avoided?

3. Do parents appreciate what it means to kids to have to change parents and families?

4. Have your real parents and stepparents been helpful to you in making family changes? How?

5. Were you happier before than after you made a family change? Why?

6. What would you like to say to parents about you or other kids having to live with new families?

CHAPTER XXV

The Single Parent

Most single parents are the product of divorce. Because there are so many single parents, one might think that they are having a hard time getting married again.

A small minority of single parents may want to be careful about getting married again soon after having failed in a previous marriage—or two or three. But that does not account for the many who remain single long after divorce. Those are the fathers and mothers who do not want to remarry. They intentionally choose to remain single.

A large number of them are single mothers who want to pursue a career to prove that they are able to support themselves and their children. It is an affirmation of their ability to succeed on their own without the help or support of a husband or any man.

That does not mean that the single mother has rejected all men in her life or that the single father has no further interest in women. Both are likely to have relationships that last for a night, a few days, weeks, or months, perhaps years.

Kids who shuttle back and forth between the separate households of their divorced parents are bound to be exposed to and involved with these new relationships of their parents. They not only have to adjust to each parent's new household and life-style, but also to their many lovers and a series of hired sitters.

Some of the suitors can be nice people, but some can be not so nice. Some may love children whereas others may hate them. Those who do not like kids will find them a nuisance to have around. They may even threaten to break off with the parent if he or she does not send the kids back to the other parent or to stay with friends or relatives.

Kids find little place for themselves in a home where the single parent works all day and spends the nights with a lover. They feel rebuffed and unwanted. Sometimes they have nowhere to go if both parents are involved in love affairs. Full of anger and resentment, many of these kids run away, get in trouble with the law, and end up in detention centers for juvenile delinquents.

On the other hand, some single parents feel so guilty about the problems they have made for their kids that they totally reject any idea of entering a new relationship. Denying themselves, they devote all their life and energy to the care and needs of their kids. Kids quickly sense this self-denial and how unhappy it makes the parent, and may try to encourage the parent to find a person she or he might love. Kids are even ready to offer their good services in searching for someone who might make Mom or Dad happy again.

It is at such times that kids can be more helpful to parents than parents can be to kids. They know what it is for Mom or Dad not to have someone to love as Mom and Dad once loved each other. They want to help as they share in the loss of love they all once had as a family.

After having to accept the hard blow that their divorced parents will never get back together again, they are able to see that a new mate must be found for the single parent and, hopefully, a good stepparent for them.

For single parents and their kids, the search to become a family again may lead to other failures. Yet it is the goal of being a family again that makes all the grief entailed in the search worthwhile.

Suggested Questions for Discussion

1. If you live with a single parent, is it your mother or father? Why?

2. Do you agree with this arrangement? Did you participate in making the arrangement?

3. How have your parents' lives changed since they separated?

4. Are they or are they not happy as single parents?

5. How do you feel about their living as single parents?

6. Does either single parent have a lover?

7. Is that person nice to you?

8. Does that person live in your home? If so, do you like the arrangement?

9. Do you frankly express your feelings to your parents about their life-style as single parents?

10. What are your ideas about the sort of life a single parent should lead?

11. Do your parents lead the kind of life you like and agree with?

12. Has the life of your single parents been a happy one for you?

CHAPTER XXVI

Kids Grow Up, Parents Grow Old

By the time you leave high school and your teen years are about over, you are ready to be on your own at college, in a training school for some specific occupation, or on a job. What you do from now on is more up to you than to your parents.

As concerns your life, what your parents have or have not done for you is over. They have served you for better or worse. If they have served you well up to this time, so much the better for you. If not, so much the worse.

If you leave home, it will create a big change for your parents. They will again be alone together as they were before they had you. But it won't be the same. For some eighteen or more years they have devoted much of their lives to you. If they were happy years as a family, it will be hard for them to see you leave. The shock of your leaving will take a long time to get over. They will miss you terribly, perhaps more than you will them as you eagerly look forward to your future. Devoted parents do not easily, if ever, give up being parents. Wherever you go, whatever you do, they will still be the same doting mother and father, and you will still be their darling little boy or girl who needs their advice and help.

The leave-taking of a kid can be even more poignant for parents who have not been getting along very well and have transferred all their affection to the kid. With him or her absent, they suddenly find themselves alone and even further isolated from each other. They no longer have someone around to talk with, to hide behind, or to be used as a bargaining chip in their relations, as kids sometimes are. It is not until the kid leaves home that they realize what they have been doing to each other and to the child.

At this time in their lives, when parents are likely to be in their 40's, the question that looms before them is, "What now?" For many parents it is like having to start all over again. They have been so involved in raising kids for so long that they have lost their bearings with each other. They have devoted so much of their time and energy to kids that they have forgotten to consider each other.

Through none of their own doing, kids can unite or divide parents by their need for constant care and attention. Especially is this true if the parents commit their every moment and their entire relationship to the kids and forget about their own needs and the love that brought them together in the first place. It is these parents who have forgotten about each other while raising kids who are at a loss when the kids leave home.

For them it becomes a painful, if not impossible, task to come together again as the spontaneous couple they once were. Having spent so many years managing kids and the household and their jobs, they find that their love for each other has been managed almost out of existence by the rigma-role of family demands. They reach for each other only if they are not too tired by the end of the day, or if the kids are not around, which is rarely the case.

The closeness of parents can also suffer by having to relate to each other mostly through their kids and the repetitive humdrum responsibilities of family life. Parents can come to relate to each other only as supervisors, custodians, accountants, taxi drivers, cooks, first-aid medics, dishwashers, tutors, bank tellers, counselors, coaches, carpenters—the list is endless.

This is also the time of life when parents reach that rumored halfway mark called "the middle-age crisis" and pause to reflect about their past and become concerned about what their future holds for them. Such a reassessment usually includes such searching questions as: What do I want the rest of my life to be like? Isn't it time to try something else in life? What about a new job, a different line of work? Perhaps a business of my own? Live in a new town or in another part of the country? Maybe even the world? Travel? Enjoy life before it is too late. What could be a better time now that the kids have all gone.

If some of these reflections are daydreams to middle-aged parents, they still represent an awareness that time is passing and that the options left for the rest of their life are becoming fewer and more remote. Worries about getting old cast a shadow as parents note that they are not as physically fit as they used to be, not as agile, not as active. There can even be concern over some actual bodily infirmities that have developed.

Parents may figure: "It took twenty years before I got married and another twenty before the kids left home. That puts me in the early or middle forties. Now there are only twenty years or so before I retire—that is, if I live that long."

Parents soon begin to think more of their own welfare than that of the kids who have left home. Who's going to take care of them if they become seriously ill or too old to take care of themselves? You can't depend on the kids. They'll have their hands too full taking care of their own families to find time to help us. Will we have enough money for our old age? Will we end up in some awful nursing home? And how will we be able to pay the charges those places demand?

Some parents, of course, block out all this worry and live only for the day. Others are so poor that there is nothing to plan for but the minimal needs of daily living—food on the table and paying the rent, light, and telephone bills.

Suggested Questions for Discussion

1. Are your parents worried about getting older?

2. What signs, if any, do they see that they are getting older?

3. Have either of your parents any illnesses or infirmities that concern them?

4. Have you been aware of your parents getting older? If you have, what are your feelings about it?

5. Do you think raising a family has been hard on your parents? Has it interfered with their love for each other?

6. Do your parents still love each other as much as they once did? If not, why not?

7. Has either of your parents experienced "the middle-age crisis"? If so, what kind of "crisis" was it? What have they done about it?

8. Do you think they will be happy when all their kids have left home so they can spend more time alone together?

9. How do they plan to use their time when the kids are no longer at home?

10. Are they looking forward to retirement? How soon will that be?

11. Do you think your parents should have planned better than they have for their future? For the family's future?

CHAPTER XXVII

What Happens to Old Parents?

Unfortunately, there is no policy or practice in our country that spells out what should be done with old parents. Since they are not considered productive members of society, they are tolerated, like the mentally retarded, out of some tenuous moral or ethical obligation that pricks the conscience of society.

Why talk to you about this? First of all, it is an important problem that you should know about if you are to understand parents, the old as well as the young. Second, it may not be long before you have to face the issue of what to do with your parents when they are old. Third, if you presently have aging grandparents, you know what it is for parents to get old. To bring this problem close to your own life, ask your parents what they think should be done with their parents when they become too old to take care of themselves. Fourth, from your own selfish viewpoint you should know that economists urge young people of your age to start putting money aside for the time when they get old. If you fail to do so now, the chances are that you will not have enough money when you get old to pay for food, rent, medical care, clothing, utilities, and other basic needs so that you can live comfortably during the last years of your life. It is predicted that by the time you retire your income from retirement funds plus Social Security will probably be insufficient to support you. Some say that Social Security will have been phased out by the time you retire. Already some old parents are having to depend on their grown children to support them if they are able. If there are no children to help, they have to depend on charity from religious and community agencies plus food stamps from the government.

Certain cultural changes have taken place over the years in our country that have made it more difficult for old parents to receive the kind of support they need and once had. When European immigrants came in droves to the United States in the late 1800's, the settlers brought with them strong religious and cultural traditions that respected old parents and guaranteed that they would be well taken care of until the day they died. That was also true of the Japanese and Chinese families who settled in America.

Old parents then were venerated and valued members of the family. They were looked upon as the source of wisdom, for they had lived long and learned much about life that could benefit the younger and less experienced members of the family. There was also a strong feeling of obligation by the grown children to repay all that their parents had done for them when they were kids. As a result, old parents never had to worry about what would happen to them when they became too old to take care of themselves.

Today, things are very different for old parents. Concern for their welfare is no longer as evident as it once was. The traditions of the early immigrants to care for aged parents are almost gone except for a few close-knit families that still retain those traditions. In our so-called modern culture, old parents are seen as old fogies, out of style, out of touch, and living in the past. On TV and radio and in advertisements, the old are seen only in caricature. Their "old ideas" and "old ways" have no place in our fast-paced society where ideas and things valued today are old and discarded by tomorrow. How can old parents have any value in a society where value is judged primarily in commercial, not human, terms? Moreover, how can the American family value old parents when it no longer values itself?

What happens to old parents in our society?

Old parents who are wealthy live comfortably, if not ele-
gantly as many do, in fancy homes and condominiums. Those
are usually located in the better neighborhoods or in private
developments designed as retirement communities. Here they
have golf courses, swimming pools, and a variety of active
physical and social programs to enjoy with others of their
own age. They have door-to-door private bus transportation
to local shopping centers. Some retirement communities also
offer supportive health and medical services as needed.

After the retirement home comes the nursing home, where
wealthy old parents go when they become too ill or too old to
take care of themselves. In these caring, but expensive, nursing homes, the very old and sick parents spend their last days.

Old parents who are poor or of middle income are not so
fortunate. Their only income is from Social Security, which
averages between $200 and $400 a month, with possibly a few
hundred dollars of retirement money. These parents can
hardly afford more than a small apartment in a lower-income
neighborhood, a room in a ghetto or slum, or a small trailer
home in the country or a trailer park. Many must live on food
stamps and handouts from charitable agencies and churches.
If their grown children have not forgotten them, they may
occasionally visit them, bring them food, and do some house-
cleaning. Sometimes old parents are completely neglected or
forgotten by their children.

If these parents cannot afford to live by themselves, they
may have to live with their married children. Such an arrangement may or may not work out. Much depends on how the
children get along with their spouses. If they argue and fight a
great deal, the last days of the old parents can become a
nightmare. They will worry about what might happen to them
if the family breaks up and there is a divorce. Where will they
go then? What will happen to them? Will they find themselves
alone and uncared for?

Even if there are no domestic problems in the house, the
married children find it harder and harder to take care of the

old parents as their health declines and they require full-time nursing and medical care. What often finally happens is that these very old and sick parents spend their last days in second- or third-rate nursing homes, the cost of which is paid by contributions from various members of the family.

It is said that a society is judged by how well or poorly it takes care of its poor, its sick, its handicapped, and its old. Each person must ask how much he or she contributes to this judgment of our society when it comes to the care of his or her old parents.

Suggested Questions for Discussion

1. What do your parents think about the role of old parents in our society?

2. What do they think should be done with old parents?

3. Have they thought much about their getting old? If not, why not?

4. Is old age a topic they would rather not discuss? If so, why?

5. Have you ever spoken to your parents about their getting old so that you might understand old age better?

6. Have your parents made any plans for their care when they are too old to take care of themselves?

7. If they have not made any plans, do they think they should?

8. Should they tell you about those plans?

9. Would they want to spend their old age living with their children? Why or why not?

10. What are your parents now doing to help their old parents, your grandparents?

11. Do they think they are doing their best to help their parents?

CHAPTER XXVIII

The Death of Parents

Like anyone else, parents can die at any time, at any age. Some die before a baby is born, while it is being born, or at any time thereafter. Parents can die suddenly from a serious accident or illness, or they can linger on for years as invalids, confined to a bed or a wheelchair. Both parents can die at the same time, or one can die while the other lives on.

Whatever the time or circumstances, the death of a parent is an emotionally upsetting event for the family. Especially is this so if the parent who died was well loved. But even if the parent was not loved, there is still sorrow, if only the sorrow of regret and guilt that life with the parent did not turn out better. The death of a cruel and ruthless parent, on the other hand, can come as a relief to a distraught family that has had to live with such a mother or father.

It is not until one parent dies that the surviving parent is deluged with memories of their life together. Ordinarily, parents recall only brief snatches of that past as they go about their daily tasks. The happenings of the present usually have greater importance. It is mostly on holidays, anniversaries, birthdays, or at other special times of family gatherings that parents recall the fond memories of their earlier lives together.

The death of a spouse, however, releases the full flood of memories in the mind of the surviving parent. Memories of their love that have lain dormant over the years suddenly surge through the grieving parent with such force that the real world is wiped out in sorrow and tears.

With the death of a spouse there also dies a part of the surviving parent that treasures all those loving memories.

They are the proof of their life together, of their love for each other. Once those die, as they do with the passage of time, so also dies their relationship. Without memories, there is no past. That is why those who have only painful memories sometimes try to block out the past with alcohol and drugs. Some even become insane to forget an unhappy past.

Psychologists refer to this period of grieving for the death of a loved one as the way the living cope with loss. It is by tears and mourning that human beings perform the painful process of uprooting the fond memories of the loved one and thus free themselves of their sadness. So must the surviving parent perform this unhappy task with the memories of the deceased spouse.

Upon completion of the grieving period, which can take days, weeks, months, and, for some parents, years, the surviving parent frees the mind of memories of the dead spouse. Their emotional power fades as time goes on until finally they become so weak that the surviving parent is ready to seek another mate.

It is a question whether husbands or wives pass through the mourning period more quickly and are sooner ready to seek a new love. There are, of course, differences due to the personality of the mourner. Those who had a strong attachment to the deceased spouse will take longer to go through the transition than the parent who is not so emotionally attached.

When children are living with a parent who has lost a spouse through death and is ready to find another mate, it is not uncommon for them to be critical of the parent for such an interest. They can make the parent feel guilty for seeking someone else so soon after the death of a parent (it could be weeks or months or even years).

Older children, even married children, can depict the surviving parent as obscene or immoral to think of sex. Actually, elderly parents may only want a close friend and companion for the remaining years of their life.

Since men have a shorter life span than women, there are more surviving mothers than fathers. Upon the death of the father, the children go into a period of mourning with the mother. How long they mourn depends primarily on how long the mother remains in mourning. Very young children who have few memories of their father will identify with the mother and grieve as long as she does. The older children, having lived with the father longer, will have their own fond memories to grieve over.

If the bereaved mother is unable to free herself of her sorrow, her prolonged grief and depression can infect the whole family so that everyone becomes sick with sadness. The grief and depression of some mothers is so profound that they are unable to carry on with the necessary tasks of running the family. Kids can be neglected and even rejected. Perhaps only the intervention of a physician or psychiatrist can remedy the mother's emotional breakdown.

Most mothers, because they think first of the welfare of the family, do not allow themselves such self-indulgence in grief as to lead to serious consequences for the family. It is their recognition of their role in sustaining the family during such times of family trauma that turns the tragedy of the death of a parent into an affirmation of life.

Suggested Questions for Discussion

1. If one of your parents died, what was the response of the surviving parent?

2. How long did it take the surviving parent to get over his or her sorrow?

3. Were any financial provisions made by your parents to protect the family in case one or both parents died? If there were none, why not?

4. Have your parents made out wills in case of death? If not, why not?

5. Have your parents told you any of the provisions of their wills? If they have not, do you think they should?

6. If your parents have told you about their wills, do you agree with the provisions? If not, why not?

7. Have your parents made any plans for the care of the family should both die at one time, say in an automobile accident?

8. What plans, if any, have your parents made for their funeral arrangements?

9. Do you think your parents have prepared you well for the possibility of their dying? If not, why not?

10. How do you think parents should prepare kids for the day parents die?

CHAPTER XXIX

The Legacy of Parents

Often it is said that we are what we experience. That is only partly true, for some experiences mean more to us and leave a greater mark on our lives than do others. Some experiences leave little or no impression on us. Why the mind should select certain experiences and not others to influence us, perhaps for life, is not always easy to understand.

The same can be said about the influence of parents on kids. Kids, by the time they grow up, have had many years of being influenced by their parents. Why, then, do certain personality behaviors and traits of one parent become more a part of a kid than those of the other parent? Friends and relatives comment on how a kid's personality is more like the mother's than the father's, or vice versa, and how a kid looks more like one than the other.

The personality and physical traits of a kid may be more like one parent than the other, but they are never perfect duplicates of either parent. There is also evident a subtle composite of both parents in every kid, even when the characteristics of one seem more prominent than those of the other. Finally, what a kid does with this legacy of parental personality and behavior traits, some inherited and others acquired, determines the kid's own distinct personality.

Usually kids are grown up before they become aware of the influence their parents have had on their personalities. Much of this awareness may initially be due more to what people say about their being like one or the other parent. It is not until kids are in their late teens or their twenties, and perhaps until they are married and have their own children, that they realize how much they really are like one or the other parent. It takes that long for them to gain perspective on the parental influences on their lives.

It also takes that long for some kids to accept those influences and be happy with them. It may be only when kids become adults that they first come to appreciate their parents for what they were and how much they really meant in their lives. All this is possible, of course, only if the parents were good parents.

Not always is it a happy awareness for kids to see themselves as like their parents. Although they may love their parents very much, they want also to be their own personal selves. That is why, for example, if a father is a creative artist, his son may want to be anything but a creative artist to establish his own individuality distinct from his father's. In his efforts to become something different from his father, say a scientist, he may nevertheless display his father's legacy by being a very creative scientist. Creativity is a common denominator in father and son no matter what form it takes and how it expresses itself.

To some kids, being like their parents and following in their footsteps is no problem at all. They do not feel that they need to be different from their parents to prove their individuality and worth. They are happy, even proud, to look like their parents, act like their parents, and even follow the profession or occupation of their parents. Some even make it a mission in life to further the work their parents have pioneered.

The picture is quite different with kids who have been left a legacy of divorce: stepparents, single parents, adoptive parents, absent parents, and parents who have deserted them. Where do these kids find their anchorage in the wild tides of relationships tossing them about, some since they were infants? Who are the adults they can learn to love and emulate when none are around long enough or have any redeeming human values to emulate? How can these kids be expected to know what it is to have one's own identity? For them it is not a question of following or not following in someone's footsteps; there are so many adults stamping all over their lives that it is impossible for them to follow or not follow, or care to follow, anyone.

The picture is equally bleak for kids whose parents have left them a legacy of hate, cruelty, anger, and drugs. These kids hate themselves because all they have known is hate. They can never know peace because they have known only anger and fighting. They are cruel because they have never had kindness. Like their parents, their lives will be corroded by drugs and drunkenness. This is the group in our society that makes up most of the population of our mental and penal institutions and those lost wanderers and beggars on our city streets.

The society kids grow up in also leaves them legacies. Will those legacies be poverty or good economic times, strife and conflict or stability and cooperation, cheap politics or statesmanship, indifference or compassion toward the less fortunate, restricted liberty or freedom and human rights?

Will it be a society under the constant threat of nuclear war or a society with the world at peace? Will it be a society that will preserve and protect or destroy the legacies of dedicated parents who have worked so hard over the years and generations to leave their kids and their kids' kids with an understanding and respect for all the peoples of the world?

Suggested Questions for Discussion

1. At this age in your life how would you sum up the legacy your parents have left you as to what they have or have not contributed to your feelings about life, yourself, your ideas, and your welfare?

2. What has your mother left you as a legacy?

3. What has your father left you as a legacy?

4. Are you satisfied with the legacy your parents have left you? Explain.

5. Do you consider yourself lucky to have the parents you have? Why or why not?

6. Are there values you have gained for yourself that are not a part of the legacy of your parents?

CHAPTER XXX

Is the Influence of Parents Slipping?

If it were not for the many years of necessary dependence on parents for care and welfare, kids would probably not be so greatly influenced by their parents as they are. That dependence is almost total during a child's formative years when it requires the complete help of the parents to feed and clothe it and take care of its physical and emotional needs. As the child grows older, it also depends upon its parents to help it learn about its immediate world, the family, and the world outside.

Years ago when the family was more of a self-contained, cohesive unit, undisturbed by the intrusions of newspapers and magazines, radio, TV, and telephone, kids knew little of the outside world. They were pretty much at the mercy of their parents for whatever they did or thought. Parents may have served as a protective shield for kids, but at the price of confining their kids' views of life to their own. This restricted and censored view of life gave the parents a control over kids that no longer exists. Placed in this historical context, the influence of parents on kids has indeed slipped.

But is that necessarily bad?

Perhaps it would be more correct to say that the absolute control of kids by their parents has been challenged to stand up to the realities of the world as kids are beginning to know them.

Where parents have slipped in their influence on kids is where they have failed in this challenge. For kids there are disturbing questions that need to be answered: Is what parents believe and think the only way to believe and think? If not, and if there are other options, what is the justification for what parents want kids to think and believe? In addition, kids are becoming more aware of the double standard between what parents want them to do and believe and what parents themselves do and believe in the world outside the home. If there is a slippage in the influence of parents on kids, how much is due to the dishonesty of parents and the resulting lack of trust by kids in parents and the adult world?

Considerable mourning has been indulged in about kids having lost the innocence of childhood through the invasion of the sanctity of the home by the harsh realities of the adult world. Whereas before, the argument goes, kids were protected from disturbing and often brutal realities of the adult world and could bask in the make-believe world of fantasy, they no longer have this world of enchantment with which to protect themselves.

Much of the so-called need to protect the innocence of kids is also the need to prevent them from learning some of the unsavory truth about their less-than-innocent parents and the adult world. Parents often express it this way: "Let the poor darlings enjoy their happy ignorance about life as long as they can. They'll soon enough learn how cruel and unkind the world really is."

A revealing contemporary example of the ultimate attempt by parents to deceive kids is their present fumbling, inept efforts to cover up the dangers of nuclear war. How can any parent honestly pretend concern over kids losing their innocence when they all may lose their lives at any moment in a nuclear holocaust?

If anything has demolished the dreams and innocence of kids and led to their disenchantment with parents, it is the breakup of the family and parents who leave kids to take all the consequences that follow from that tragedy. None of the possible negative consequences of radio, TV, movies, computers, or loss of innocence that parents fear can compare to what separation and divorce do to kids.

Neither do kids need parents who shirk their responsibility

by turning their job over to squads of surrogate parents such as teachers, counselors, psychologists, psychiatrists, and state and county family aid agencies to do what parents themselves failed to do.

Suggested Questions for Discussion

1. Do you think the influence of parents on kids is slipping? Explain why or why not.

2. Do you think divorce and the breakup of families have diluted or even negated the influence of parents on kids?

3. What should kids do during this time when so many marriages are falling apart?

4. Do you think kids believe that parents are more of a problem than a help to them? Explain.

5. Can kids trust parents to be honest and truthful with them? Why or why not?

6. How many parents of your friends do you admire and respect? Why do you admire them?

7. Do you admire and respect your own parents? Why or why not?

8. How do you feel parents can help kids the most?

9. What kind of person must a parent be to win a kid's admiration and respect?

10. What sense do you get from kids you know about how important the influence of parents is on them today?

11. Are kids looking to other than their parents as models to admire and emulate? If so, why? Who are those models?

12. Do those models deserve any more respect and admiration than parents? Why or why not?

CHAPTER XXXI

How Do Your Parents Stand?

By the time you have come to this last chapter, you have probably gained a good idea where your mother and father stand as parents and fellow human beings from the many questions you have discussed with them at the end of each chapter.

The final and important question that gives the main value to the book, if it has any value at all, is: "Do you now have a better understanding of parents, especially your own parents, than you had before you read this book?" If not, the book has failed and I, as the author, have failed also.

As you probably surmised near the beginning, this is not a formula book with recipes to enable you to get along with your parents and they with you. Its basic purpose is to start you on the way to developing some insight into your parents and thus having a foundation on which to build a better relationship with them. It is always easier and more productive to work out a good relationship with someone you understand than with someone you do not understand or care for.

Remember, too, that you'll probably be a parent yourself some day. The shoe will then be on the other foot, and it will be your turn to prove your worth to your own kids.

To do a good job with kids is to be a good parent. Good, but not necessarily perfect, if there ever can be such a parent. Perfection is not a common characteristic among human beings. It is more of a hope than a reality for most people. In any case, it is not needed to be a successful parent.

A distinction should be made between what a parent is at home and what a parent is in the outside world. There are and have been parents who are famous scholars, scientists, presidents, businessmen, artists, and athletes, who are tops in their fields in the outside world but failures in their own homes. Each parent has his or her own strengths and weaknesses. But parents are rightly expected to be good parents, for that is their main job and their responsibility to the children they brought into the world. Too many parents, unfortunately, worry more about being failures in the outside world than about failing as parents in their own home.

What is a good parent? There is a lot of talk about the basics in school, such as math, science, and English, that every student must master if he or she can be said to be a good student. What are the basics that a parent must master to be considered a good parent? She or he must be capable in three basic areas: as a person, as a marriage partner, and as a parent. The first two are prerequisites to becoming a good parent. A parent who takes pride in being called a parent is a fraud if he or she has not first demonstrated mastery of these basics at least to a tolerable degree of competency; say, better than a C.

Of course, as with students so with parents, there is always room for improvement. Why can't kids tell parents, "Try harder"? Isn't that what parents keep telling their kids?

Appendix

Where and How to Get Help

Whether it is for yourself, a member of your family, or your entire family, that you would like advice and help with problems, the best place to start is with the resources that exist in your own community. For yourself, perhaps there is a teacher in whom you can confide with trust and confidence. The school guidance counselor and the school psychologist are professionally trained to help students with personal and academic problems. If you belong to a church or synagogue, you can call on the minister, the priest, or the rabbi. Your family physician or an adult friend or relative might be able to help. If none of these feel that they can help, perhaps they can direct you to someone who can.

If these resources fail, it will be up to you to explore the available resources in your town or city. Check with your state Department of Social and Health Services and the Department of Licensing to be sure that any organizations or person you plan to consult has been approved and licensed by the state. These offices and others are listed in the yellow pages of the phone book under some such title as the following:

    I. Social Service Organizations
   II. Mental Health Services
 III. Marriage, Family, Child, and Individual Counselors
 IV. Social Workers

I. *Social Service Organizations*

These are lay organizations or religious, welfare, or governmental groups that serve the public without a fee or at a minimal fee. The advantage of such groups is their experience in working with the public. Most are licensed by the state and are reliable and legitimate organizations that will respect your need for confidentiality. Many are also associated with national organizations.

You should phone the appropriate organization for an appointment to explore your needs and find out what specifically they may be able to do to help you.

The following are examples of organizations commonly found in large urban areas:

Alliance for Youth and Families
American Friends Service Committee
American Red Cross
American Council for the Blind
Autistic Children Society
Big Brothers
Cancer Counseling and Education
CARE
Catholic Community Services
Center for the Prevention of Sexual Abuse and
    Domestic Violence
Center for the Retarded
Child Abuse Center
Child Guidance Center
Children's Home Society
Chinese Information and Service Center
Community Psychiatric Clinic
Community Service for the Deaf and Hard of Hearing
Consejo Counseling and Referral Service
Counseling Center
Crisis Clinic
Divorce Lifeline
Easter Seal Society for Crippled Children and Adults
Epilepsy Association

Freedom from Abuse Center
Group Homes
Help Line
International District Community Health Center
Jewish Family Service
Lutheran Social Services
Mental Health Institute
Multiple Sclerosis Association
Neighborhood Health Center
Parent Education Services
Parent Phone Line
Youth Services Bureau

II. *Mental Health Services*

Community mental health centers and psychiatric and psychological services are located in the various sections and neighborhoods of urban areas.

These can be run by the city, county, or state. Many are private, especially the psychological and psychiatric services. Some are associated with hospitals and universities. They may include parent and family counseling. Some charge fees on a sliding scale.

Therapies for specific disabilities are among the spectrum of services provided under the heading Mental Health Services. They include:

Individual and group psychiatric treatment
Family therapy
Psychological and educational testing
Vocational and educational counseling
Behavior therapy
Remediation of emotional and/or adjustment problems
Academic programs for the learning disabled
Hearing and speech disorders
Reading and language problems

Sensory-motor dysfunction
Perceptual-motor disabilities
Emotionally disturbed, autistic, and psychiatric children
Drug abuse
Mentally retarded
Coping with crisis situations
Parental and marital counseling

III. *Marriage, Family, Child, and Individual Counselors*
Yellow pages sample titles include:

Adolescent and Adult Drug and Alcohol Clinic
Adolescent and Family Program
Adult and Child Therapy Center
Associate Counseling and Therapy Services
Associates in Psychology
Catholic Community Services
Child Therapy Association
Community Services
Counseling Center
Counseling for Relationships and New Family Ways
Divorce Lifeline
Family Crisis Service for Immediate Assistance
Family Services
Lutheran Counseling Network
Parent Place
Presbyterian Counseling Service
Unitarian Counseling Associates
Women's Counseling Group

IV. *Social Workers*

Depending on their training and specialization, social workers can be very effective in many problem areas in human relations. They are particularly helpful in finding supportive aids and resources in the community to assist with the everyday problems of life at school, in the home, and in the community.

Those who are accredited and most reliable use after their name an MSW (Master of Social Work) degree or an ACSW (member of the Academy of Certified Social Workers) from the professional organization of social workers. Ask about services and fees. If interested, request an exploratory interview.

Government Services—City

Under the name of your town or city in the white pages of the phone directory:

A. *Health Services*
   Children and Youth Clinic
   Personal Health Services

B. *Department of Human Resources*
   Youth Services

Government Services—County

Under the name of your county in the white pages of the phone directory:

A. *Health Services*
   Personal Health Services
   County Service Centers (choose the one nearest your home

B. *Department of Human Resources*
   Community Service Division
   Human Services Division

Government Services—State

Under the name of your state in the white (or blue) pages of the phonebook:

A. *Social and Health Services*
   Child Protective Services
   Family Reconciliation Services (24-hour service)
   Community Services Office
   (Choose the one nearest your neighborhood)
B. *Department of Mental Health*
C. *Department of Rehabilitation and Handicapped Children*
D. *Department of Human Resources*

Legal Services

If you need legal advice or referral to appropriate legal help, contact the American Civil Liberties Union or the Lawyers Guild. While they do not do legal work for older adolescents, they will direct you to attorneys who protect juvenile rights. Both of these are national organizations with local offices in most large cities. The United Way Agency, found in most communities, can also direct you to legal help. Some organizations that serve as legal advocates (in some places known as Youth Advocates) can not only inform older kids of their basic rights but also serve as shelters when kids run away from home to escape physical harm or mental cruelty.

Family Violence

With the growing enactment of state and local laws that prohibit violence of parent against parent and parent against children in the home, the police can now enter a home and arrest and jail offenders.

If violence occurs in your home, or if there is serious danger of violence in your home, phone the police or dial 911 (emergency) immediately. If you are unable to do so in your home, go to your neighbors and use their phone.

A 1984 report by a federal Task Force on Family Violence urges immediate action by state and local authorities to stop the large and growing number of crimes of violence being committed in the home.

The home can no longer be called "a man's castle" where the violent can take refuge from the law. Now the violent behavior of any of its members can be called to account.

The Attorney General of the United States said, on presenting the report, that family crime should be treated as seriously as street crime. "Child abuse, spouse abuse, and the abuse of the elderly, incest and child molestation are not a matter of personal belief on how to deal with children or keep order in the house," said the report. "They are crimes. They are prohibited."

The report recommended that:

1. People charged with violent family crimes be arrested as if there were no relationship between the victim and the alleged attacker.
2. When no arrest is warranted, the investigating officer file a report on an incident.
3. Prosecutors cease requiring victims to sign a formal complaint against a close relative to initiate prosecution.
4. Victimized children be handled with greater sensitivity by prosecutors and judges. The report proposed videotaping the testimony of children so they do not have to confront their attackers in the courtroom.
5. Judges jail violent abusers who inflict serious injury. "When appropriate," the report said, "judges should have the option of imposing weekend or evening jail sentences to preserve a family's financial stability."